NORTHERN EXPOSURE™

The Official Publication of the Television Series

by

Louis Chunovic

Based on the Universal Television series
Northern Exposure
Created by Joshua Brand & John Falsey

A CITADEL PRESS BOOK
Published by Carol Publishing Group

A Citadel Press Book
Published by Carol Publishing Group

Citadel Press is a registered trademark of Carol Communications, Inc.

Editorial Offices: 600 Madison Avenue, New York, N.Y. 10022
Sales & Distribution Offices: 120 Enterprise Avenue, Secaucus, N.J. 07094
In Canada: Canadian Manda Group, P.O. Box 920, Station U, Toronto,
Ontario M8Z 5P9

Queries regarding rights and permissions should be addressed to
Carol Publishing Group, 600 Madison Avenue, New York, N.Y. 10022

Carol Publishing Group books are available at special discounts
for bulk purchases, for sales promotions, fund raising, or educational
purposes. Special editions can be created to specifications.
For details contact: Special Sales Department, Carol Publishing Group,
120 Enterprise Avenue, Secaucus, N.J. 07094

Photos courtesy of CBS.
Photos courtesy Mary Ellen Seaman.

Manufactured in the United States of America
10   9   8   7   6   5   4   3   2   1

Designed by Paul and Dolores Gamarello/Eyetooth Design Inc.

Library of Congress Cataloging-in-Publication Data

Chunovic, Louis.
    The Northern exposure book : the official publication of the
television show / by Louis Chunovic.
        p.   cm.
    "A Citadel press book."   ISBN 0–8065–1409–4
    1. Northern exposure (Television program)   I. Northern exposure
(Television program)   II. Title.
PN1992.77.N67C58   1993
791.45′72—dc20
                                                            92–37562
                                                            CIP

CONTENTS

ACKNOWLEDGMENTS

My thanks to the creators, cast, and crew of *Northern Exposure* for their cooperation with and courtesy to an inquisitive stranger in their midst, and to Anne Tschida for her expert editorial assistance.

INTRODUCTION

Like the multi-Emmy-winning television series it chronicles, this is a book for adults and for those of any age who like their whimsy mixed with intelligence and wit, but who also wonder what makes the magic work.

For here you will find real life, real people, and the real professionals who create *Northern Exposure*, one of the most engaging and best crafted series ever to air on prime time television.

A visitor with unimpeded access to a successful series shooting on a distant location continues to be a relative rarity. But this particular visitor—a longtime professional journalist on the Hollywood beat—had that kind of access to the real denizens of the fictional Cicely, Alaska, at a time of high drama for the show itself:

It was the late summer and early fall of 1992, and Rob Morrow, the young actor who portrays Dr. Joel Fleischman, had just gone through a very public and very risky renegotiation of his contract. There had been tough talk on both sides. Moreover, the show was dealing with the pressures of acclaim; it led all others in the upcoming Emmy nominations, eventually winning the awards for Outstanding Drama and Supporting Actress (for Valerie Mahaffey, who plays the recurring ditzy hypochondriac, Eve), as well as the Emmys for writing, cinematography, editing, and art direction.

Also, shooting was just underway on the first episodes since the show had gotten a nearly unprecedented fifty-episode order from the network. In other words, the stakes had never been higher, the spotlight never hotter.

The creators and the producers of *Northern Exposure* nonetheless sent out the word: cooperate with the kid.

What follows is an attempt to do something rarely done in a behind-the-scenes book. Because you, the *Northern Exposure* fan, *found* the series for yourself—without the usual hype—and remain attracted to it for its intelligence and wit, you won't be forced to endure hype here either. But your curiosity will be satisfied and you will find an unfiltered report: This is what it's *really* like.

***

Northern Exposure is Appointment TV. In the Biz that's what they call it. It's the Holy Grail in the Hollywood network-television world today.

"Appointment TV" is not simply must-watch series television, although it most assuredly is that. In an era of fragmented audiences and increased viewer choices an "appointment" network hit is one that snares those younger, hipper, busier, or better-off viewers, those who rarely have the time—or the desire—to sit down in front of the tube. People who do talk about it at school or around the water cooler at the office the next morning.

These days, that's increasingly rare. But ever since it debuted as a short-run summer replacement, people have been talking to their sometimes dubious friends about *Northern Exposure*, cherishing its oddball cast of expertly drawn regulars and oohing 'n' aahing over enchanting (and enchanted) Cicely, picturesque hamlet on the "Alaskan Riviera," temporary home of that most unwilling fish-out-of-water, dyed-in-the wool Manhattan yuppie Joel Fleischman, M.D.

Why?

From the beginning, the series was characterized by exceptional writing. The vivid, eccen-

tric characters and their intersecting, always slightly out-of-phase stories combined real-life, in-your-face specificity with charming Cicely's universal and timeless appeal.

We're talking about a town, current population about 870, with a great radio station out of a store front and an unbeatable jukebox in the local bar; a town founded in the middle of the wilderness by those emancipated turn-of-the century lesbians, Roslyn and Cicely, where the current chief civic booster is a blustery ex-astronaut with a penchant for real-estate schemes and Broadway show tunes, and where the mail is delivered by a plucky female bush pilot, late of Gross Pointe, Michigan, whose assorted boyfriends keep meeting untimely (and wildly unlikely) fates; an idyllic place on the Last Frontier, where May-December romances flower, spirits roam, and the town doctor is an unwilling hostage to a medical-school loan.

Not surprisingly, given just how offbeat it is, when *Northern Exposure* debuted in the summer of 1990, it had only a tiny eight-episode order from CBS. After all, dubious network programming executives thought they were getting *St. Elsewhere*-on-the-tundra, a natural enough assumption given that *Northern Exposure* was cre-

ated by Joshua Brand and John Falsey, the young, respected writing-producing team that also had given us the much-admired, but relatively little-watched, Boston teaching-hospital docs 'n' drama show, among others.

Largely on the strength of Emmy-venerated *St. Elsewhere*, Brand and Falsey were known inside the business as expert purveyors of quality hour-long dramas. Who knew the guys could do comedy, too?

Not the Academy of Television Arts and Sciences, which hands out the Emmys and annually is afflicted with category-itis. As he and John Falsey accepted *Northern Exposure*'s Emmy for Outstanding Dramatic Series at the Academy's 44th annual award show in 1992, Josh Brand quipped, "Well, I guess we can reveal it to them now, that we really are a comedy."

More than most shows, *Northern Exposure* was a populist, as well as popular, hit. The show "built" its loyal audience through word-of-mouth and positive reviews. So, by the time a visitor arrived in Rosyln, the picturesque Washington town that doubles as Cicely, hundreds and hundreds of tourists a day were making the pilgrimage to watch their favorite series shoot.

NORTHERN EXPOSURE

THE SHOOT

ROSLYN

Eighty-some picturesque miles out of *tres*-hip Seattle, capital of grunge rock, an hour-and-a-half east on I-90 as it cuts through the majestic, greenwood-covered Cascade Mountains, hard by the old-growth splendors of the Snoqualmie Alpine Wilderness National Forest lies tiny Roslyn, Washington, population eight hundred or so, altitude 2,266 feet, a little coal-and-timber town that thought it had seen its heyday back in the twenties, before the local mines played out.

Then one summer day, the magic makers from Hollywood came around.

All of a sudden, tiny Roslyn—with its boxy, wood-frame houses and single main street like something out of an Old West daguerreotype—is a tourist destination. It's where they film the exteriors for *Northern Exposure*. It's...

Cicely, Alaska.

HONEYMOON IN CICELY

People come daily by the hundreds to see Cicely whenever the show's in town. They even drive cross-country to honeymoon here. Take the lovey-dovey young couple that pulls into town at about the same time as a visitor from L.A. one late-summer morning: They're student fans of the show who got to snuggling in front of a flickering TV set in a common room of their college dorm. Pretty soon, during one summer vacation, they got hitched. What do you suppose Chris-in-the-Morning (Cicely's local deejay) would make of *that*?

The newlyweds seem to be up on all the latest *Northern Exposure* gossip and trivia: the effects of sudden success on young actors, hitherto unknowns; who had just dumped his girlfriend and why; the way certain plotlines have imitated the actors' real lives, like veteran performer Barry Corbin finding out he had a grown daughter—a

"lovechild," as the tabloids would say—and his character, Maurice the ex-astronaut, learning that *he'd* fathered a son in Korea as well; the highly publicized Rob Morrow (Dr. Joel) contract renegotiations, which have just been successfully concluded; the show's sixteen Emmy nominations (leading all other series), including one for Outstanding Drama; the network's recent fifty-episode order—highly unusual in the prevailing network economic climate—and so on and so on.

The lovebirds are disappointed not to see the show's regulars strolling down Pennsylvania, the town's single main street, dominated by the Brick (Holling's bar in the show), and the famous Rosyln's Cafe palm-and-camel-oasis sign.

But the visitor, who's carrying that day's cast-and-crew call sheet, assures them that all their favorites will be in town very early the next morning, along with a big production crew.

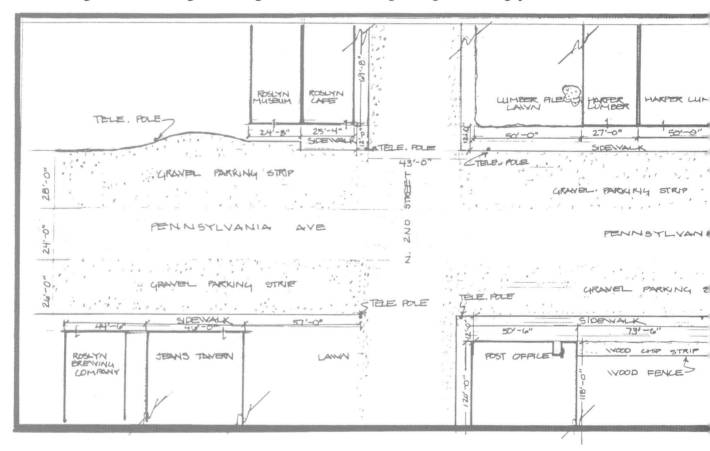

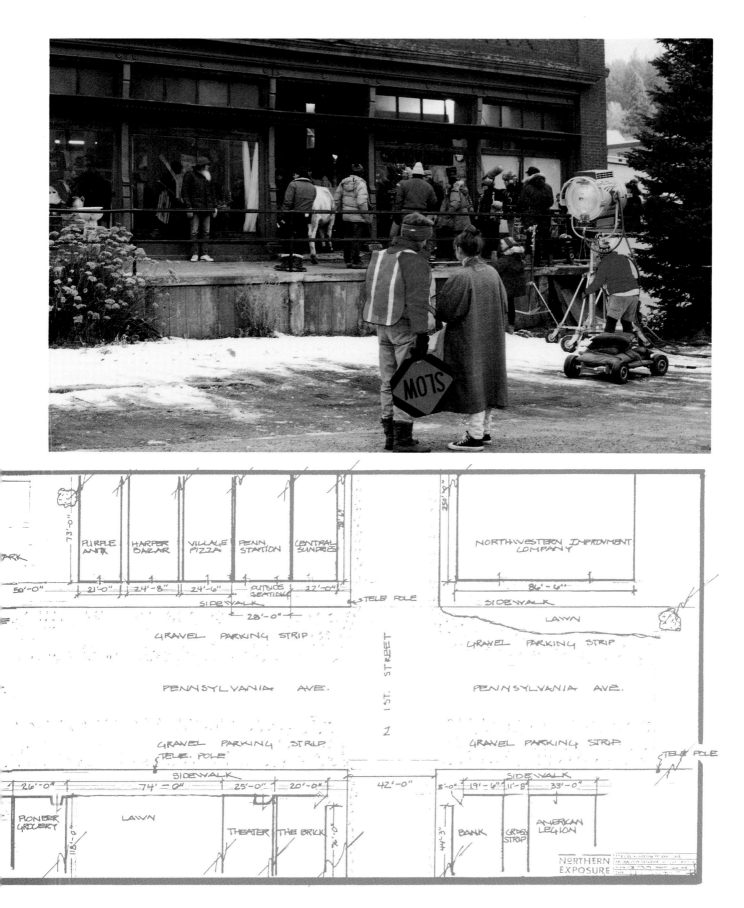

THE BUBBLE AT THE CIRCLE 8

Today, though, they're shooting on the Circle 8 Ranch, just east of Easton, a neighboring hamlet in the bosky foothills of northern Kittitas County.

A glade-like clearing in the Circle 8's pine woods is where they've built The Bubble, home to a new continuing character, lawyer Mike Monroe, whose immune system is so beleaguered by environmental degradation that he's forced to abandon his lucrative practice and move into a Buckminster Fuller-like dome outside Cicely, which, not surprisingly, turns out to be the most environmentally pristine town in all of North America.

The company is shooting exteriors around the newly built geodesic dome. It's the most complex set the art department has turned out since constructing the turn-of-the-century version of Cicely's main street for the Emmy-winning, third-season-ending episode titled "Cicely," which flashed back to tell the story of Roslyn and Cicely, the town's lesbian founders, their literary friend Franz Kafka, and the salonification of the Last Frontier.

Today's episode, though, is titled "Blowing Bubbles," and as the visitor turns in at the Circle 8 gate off Nelson Siding Road, the company is setting up for scenes that will introduce Mike Monroe, played by actor Anthony Edwards (Tom Cruise's sidekick in *Top Gun*).

Ed's first grocery delivery to the Dome, from the Prologue, and the first time Maggie meets Mike, early in Act Two, are the scenes on the schedule. The scenes shoot out of narrative order, with the Maggie-Mike meeting shooting first. This is how Maggie's first scene with Mike plays on the page:

EXT. BUBBLE—DAY Maggie approaches with a large box of supplies, stops, watches.

MAGGIE'S POV—BUBBLE Inside, Mike runs on a treadmill.

ON SCENE Mike notices Maggie and stops, drapes a towel around his neck. Maggie steps forward.

> MAGGIE
> Mike Monroe?

> MIKE
> (filtered through speaker throughout exchange)
> And you are?

> MAGGIE
> Maggie, Maggie O'Connell. I brought your mail, some supplies.

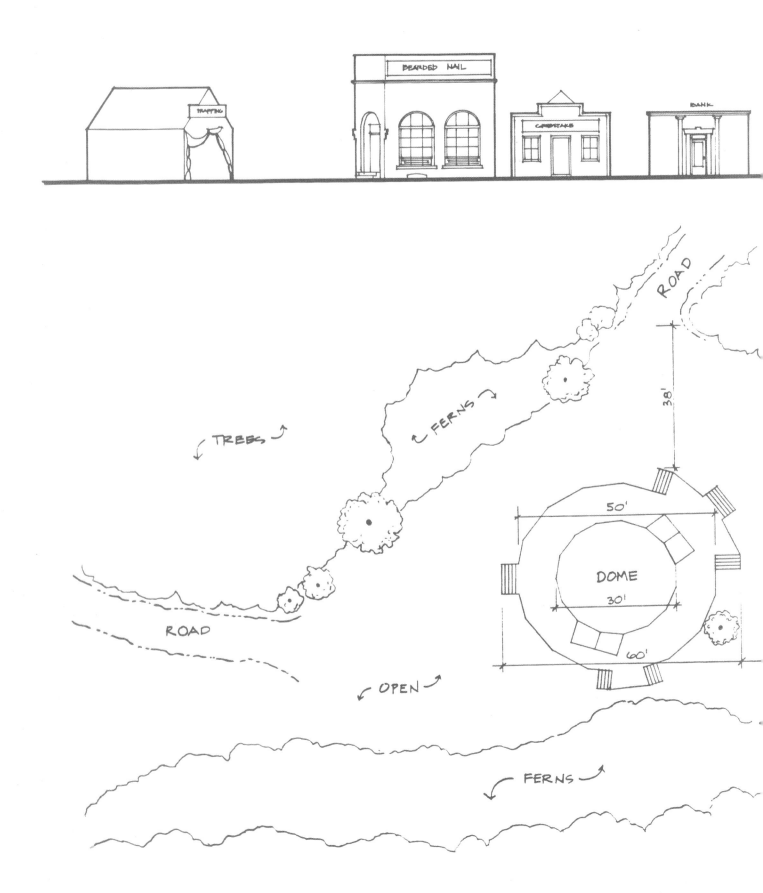

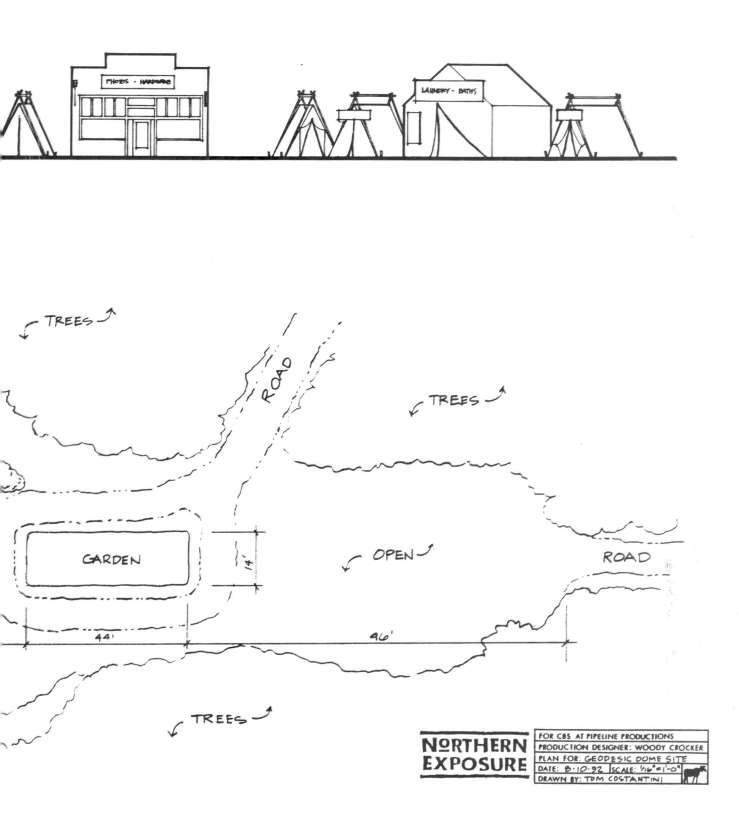

TREES

ROAD

TREES

GARDEN

14'

OPEN

ROAD

44'

96'

TREES

NORTHERN EXPOSURE

FOR CBS AT PIPELINE PRODUCTIONS
PRODUCTION DESIGNER: WOODY CROCKER
PLAN FOR: GEODESIC DOME SITE
DATE: 8·10·92   SCALE: 1/16"=1'-0"
DRAWN BY: TOM COSTANTINI

N

PHOTOS · HARDWARE

LAUNDRY · BATHS

MIKE
Where's Ed?

MAGGIE
Oh, I came right from the airport. I'm a pilot.

MIKE
Mind coming in with that? I can't go out.

MAGGIE
Fine.

MIKE
You wearing any makeup?

MAGGIE
Eyeliner...

MIKE
Perfume, shampoo, conditioner?

MAGGIE
Baby shampoo.

MIKE
How about synthetic clothing?

MAGGIE
(of jacket)
...I think this shell has some nylon in it.

MIKE
Just leave it on the hook, please.

She does, picks up the box, enters.

It looks simple, but it's not. Even to someone who's spent some time behind the scenes in Tinseltown, and hung out on more than one set, the sheer pace at which an hour weekly series is produced—120 to 130 or so people cranking twelve, fourteen, sixteen hours a day, sometimes six days a week, to turn out a mini-movie every seven or eight days, week after week during the shooting season—the complexity of the effort continues to be dazzling. The scripts are mostly wonderful, true enough; still, how *do* these people do it?

THE CO-EXECUTIVE PRODUCER

Lanky and laconic, Rob Thompson, co-executive producer and director of this episode, shrugs. "This is a pretty standard-issue script in terms of its breakdown," he explains as Janine Turner, looking pert and perfect, just like Maggie O'Connell, arrives at the location in a minivan with tinted windows. A compact, dapper, extremely self-possessed man, wearing a rather dashing brown-leather Fedora, who turns out to handle on-location security, gallantly offers his hand as she steps lightly out of the van to cries of "Yo, Janine" and wolf whistles from the crew.

Shooting the fifty-seven-page Mark Perry script (short by *Northern Exposure* standards) means "six days back at the studio," actually a converted warehouse in a Seattle suburb, Thompson continues, "one day at the Bubble, and one day in Roslyn." He eyes the bustle of activity:

Makeup and wardrobe women converging on Janine to gossip with her about their weekends, handing her a jacket and dabbing powder on her nose all the while...

Muscled grips wheeling an Apollo crane into place...

The Camera Operator peering through the lens of his Arriflex 35...

Carpenters pounding nails into the Bubble's frame...

The craft-services lady laying out a spread of snacks and sodas on a table nearby...

Stand-ins for the actors "blocking" the shot...

Held in practically every hand or slung on practically every belt is a walkie-talkie or a cellular phone; it's how this particular video army communicates in the field.

Their crackling voices are constantly conferring over camera angles and movements, pacing and lighting, and scores of other details. The camera operator, the first and second assistant directors, grips, gaffers and soundpeople, among others, execute their instructions, making certain "talent" is in place, "background" extras are ready to stroll through the shot, the crane is ready to rise, the camera is prepared to tilt.

"So this is nice," Thompson opines. "Sometimes people get bored with shooting in the soundstage. We get to go out and sort of camp out for a few days, so to speak, and when we get tired of that, we go back to the studio."

JANINE BREAKS INTO SONG

"We printed anything yet this morning?" asks the blond-haired woman who is the second second assistant director.

"Nope." Thompson lopes away, taking his place behind a Panasonic video monitor, where he can see what the camera sees, but only in a grainy black-and-white.

"Have Janine go to one when she can, please," a disembodied voice crackles over the second second A.D.'s walkie-talkie. "Let me know when we're ready outside."

"Janine is walking to her number-one position," the second second A.D. replies.

Moving to her mark below the Bubble's front steps, with the camera ready to track with her to the door, Janine Turner breaks into song. "Lover-ly, lover-ly," she trills, doing a fair imitation of Audrey Hepburn, an actress she faintly resembles, in *My Fair Lady*. "Wooouldn't it be lover-ly?"

"Okay, clear it out please," calls out the second second A.D., and the carpenters move away from the shot.

"Here we go. We are ..."

"Here we go! Quiet please! And very still! People on the deck, please—"

"Sound speed!"

"Ssshhh!!"

"Marker."

A stagehand steps up and clacks a striped clapboard in front of the camera lens. *Scene 17, Take 1.*

"Quiet, please."

"And..."

"Action, Janine."

Maggie O'Connell, wide-eyed with wonder at the geodesic dome in the middle of the wilderness, walks up the steps to the wooden deck, goes to the door and calls

out, "Mike Monroe? It's Maggie, Maggie O'Connell. I, I brought your mail, some supplies.... Well, I came straight from the airport, I'm a pilot.... Fine....Eyeliner....Baby shampoo....The shell has some nylon in it...."

"CUT!"

THE DIRECTOR OF PHOTOGRAPHY

Director of photography Frank Prinzi is just weeks away from winning his first Emmy, though of course he doesn't know it yet, for the episode titled "Cicely," whose look was consciously patterned after the classic Robert Altman anti-Western, *McCabe and Mrs. Miller*. Prinzi is a New Yorker from the get-go: sallow-complected, fast-talking, and fast-walking, with a Jim Morrison mane of shoulder-length, wavy black hair. His sincere belief that *no-way* will he win mixed with his obvious desire to is endearing.

Throughout the day, he and producer-director Thompson (who, some months later, will win the Directors Guild award for "Cicely") are constantly in conference around the video monitor.

"I work the shots with the director," he says. "I'll go to Rob or whoever [and say], 'What if we start the camera here, the actor walks forward and we dolly left as the actor goes over to the microscope?' Then, it's in [to] a close-up. Okay, then we have to intercut:

"We'll do a single [shot] on his face, while he's looking into the microscope and then [we] cut to the door and we'll see, say, Holling come in.

"We'll bring Holling in to a two shot, then dolly back or something. So what we do is, we choreograph to the story. Everything's focused on, what are we trying to show the audience? What we try to be *is* the audience."

Later, they'll shoot the "reverse," intercutting Mike Murphy's lines, but first they've got to get this shot of Maggie at the door, which in TV seems to mean shooting it again…and again…and again…

JANINE AND THE BLUE JAY

Thompson moves over to Janine, whispers a few words to her. She listens intently and nods. As Thompson walks away, the first A.D. says over the walkie-talkie: "Okay, let's go right away."

"Clearing out the front door, please!" a second A.D. shouts.

"Okay, clear, let's go guys! Doors are shut!"

"Let me know if you hear a plane lifting," asks another voice over the radio.

"Clearing..."

"Here we go."

"Is that a plane?" the sound man wants to know.

Several of the crew point upward, into the top branches of a birch tree. "It's a blue jay!"

"Fifteen seconds to rolling!"

"You want to tell Janine to find some shade. We're now fifteen seconds from rolling..."

It's an unseasonably hot day. Makeup will run, time will be wasted.

Janine steps back into the shade, but her eyes light up. "Look, a blue jay," she says, pointing delightedly. The makeup woman, who doesn't seem to be impressed, follows Janine's gaze upward.

"Twelve seconds from rolling."

"Twelve seconds and counting."

"ACK! ACK!" Janine demonstrates the sound blue jays make.

"It's a horrible noise. They go after my dog. That's how I know."

"Very impressive," the makeup woman mutters, swirling a brush across the actress's cheek.

"Lock it up!"

"Here we go! Very quiet please."

"Sshh! Sshh! Sshh!"

"Very still on the deck, please."

The makeup and wardrobe women, the car-

penters and grips and lighting technicians are momentarily a frozen tableau.

"Janine all ready there?"

"Yes she is," the second second A.D. replies.

"ROLLING!"

"Sshh!"

"ROLLING!"

"Speed!"

"And...*Action Janine!*"

They do it again.

THE STAND-INS

Dr. Joel's double is standing in for Ed Chigliak, blocking the next shot.

That is, Peter White—who himself has leading-man good looks and wears a gray Stetson hat, and has been the stand-in and double for Rob Morrow (Dr. Joel) since the pilot—is standing in for actor Darren E. Burrows, who plays Ed, while the camera and lighting people "block" the next shot, in which Ed arrives for the first time at the Dome with groceries from Ruth-Anne's for Mike.

"Blocking means hitting their marks," says White, referring to exact spots in a particular scene where actors are to stand, "what path they took, their body position, what they did first and where they did it and on which line."

He not only blocks for Morrow and Burrows, but for Barry Corbin (ex-astronaut Maurice Minnifield) and most of the other male cast members as well. "Rob's five-ten," he says, "Barry's about six, Darren's in between." That's a two-inch "stretch" for the five-foot-ten White when he's holding his position while the lights are being adjusted and the camera's being focused.

For petite, twenty-three-year-old Emily Force, a recent local drama student, who stands in for Janine Turner and the other women on the set, her work "makes life easier for the actors and the camera crew, so that once the rehearsal has been done, and they've set up the shot...the actors can go away and learn lines and get their makeup done and all that."

Not to think of herself as the star is "one of the easiest things [because Janine]...is a hell of a lot better at doing what she does than what I do," she says. "I'm so new at this that it does take all of my concentration to know where I'm supposed to be, to get there in time."

DELIVERING THE GROCERIES

The scene, which will be the prologue, only takes a few seconds on screen, but it will take hours to film:

Ed's pickup pulls into view and parks in front of the amazing Dome. He gets out—agog, slack-jawed at the sight—and heads up to the door with bags of groceries in his arms. He rings the intercom.

"Mike Monroe?" he calls out.

"Yes," replies a voice inside.

"I'm Ed....From Ruth-Anne's store."

"Right. I'm on the phone right now, Ed. You want to bring those inside?"

"Sure."

"You'll find surgical scrubs inside the door. One size fits all. I'll be with you in a moment."

"...Okay."

"Oh, and try not to touch anything," Mike's off-screen voice adds. "Thanks."

Ed nods solemnly, opens the door, stands a beat, then steps inside.

On the home screen, as the scene fades out, David Schwartz's infectious theme music begins.

ED'S PURPLE HIGH-TOPS AND MAGGIE'S ORANGE TRUCK

Wearing Ed Chigliak's purple high-top tennis shoes, Darren Burrows bounds out of the minivan that brings the actors from their trailers at the base camp, a five-minute stroll through the woods away, and runs through the shot, which begins with the truck pulling to a stop.

The grips have laid a track athwart Ed's parked Chevy truck for the gliding Arriflex camera, dollying past, and as Burrows hops out, two of them jump up and down on the back bumper to simulate the truck's coming-to-a-stop.

Then, as Ed takes the box of groceries out of the truck bed and heads up the Dome's wooden stairs, the camera turns to follow him.

The sequence is shot again and again, then Ed's Chevy is replaced by Maggie's orange Ford truck, and the Arriflex is mounted on a Chapman crane that swoops with silent grace for an over-the-shoulder shot of Maggie at the Bubble door.

"A lot of well-written scripts just tell you the story," director of photography Prinzi observes. "The shots are us."

ANNE THE ANIMAL WRANGLER AND MORT THE MOOSE

If you saw the *Northern Exposure* pilot episode, you saw Anne Gordon's on-screen debut: she was the outdoorsy Beaver Lady with the other prospective patients in the waiting room, who asks the newly arrived (and horrified) Dr. Joel Fleischman to look at her pet's teeth.

She's also a veteran animal handler, who's "wrangled" porcupines, rats, beavers, dogs, and bears for various episodes. Today, she's brought a deer and the deer's baby out on location— "They're just gonna kinda be hanging out around the Bubble"—and the crew oohs and ahhs at the ultra-cute creatures.

She's been with the show since Day One, when her first task was to find a young moose for the opening-credit sequence.

The moose she finally found was at Washington State University and was named Mort.

"He was a yearling at the time," she recalls. "He'd been bottle raised, he was an orphan out of Alaska."

For the opening sequence, "we actually fenced off the whole town of Roslyn, basically turned him loose and lured him around with bananas and willow leaves," she says.

For his day's work, Mort earned a cool $5,000, according to Anne the Animal Wrangler. Dogs make $150 a day, while bears get $500, so why did Mort do so well?

"Because he's the only working moose in the business," she explains with a laugh.

MISTER ON-LOCATION SECURITY MAN

On the side of the small Panasonic video monitor, through which Rob Thompson and Frank Prinzi view the day's shooting, a wag has taped a faded Polaroid snapshot of three men:

Actor Rob Morrow faces in one direction, Prinzi faces in the opposite direction and a third man—the same compact, dapper man who earlier had offered Janine Turner his hand as she stepped out of the minivan—stands between them facing the camera. Underneath the snapshot someone has scrawled a caption:

"Rumor has it…Emmy nominee Rob Morrow and Emmy nominee Frank Prinzi refuse to work without a Cockney bodyguard present."

A Cockney bodyguard?!

"That would be John White," advises a passing grip, who mutters, apropos of nothing. "We're still trying to figure out how we're going to fling this Bubble."

John White, formerly of the British army, stands at approximately parade rest at the edge of the action. When, between takes, actor Darren Burrow playfully throws a few punches in his direction, White slips them with tiny, subtle movements and an ingratiating smile. He is, in fact, the show's on-location security man.

He is also, a visitor learns later, a fourth degree Black Belt in Aikido, and has another Black Belt in Weapons. He's taught martial arts to the British army and American police personnel. Currently, he's vice president of International Protection Services, Ltd.

"He's this extremely mild-mannered, polite British gentleman," is how one crew member describes him.

His grip is viselike and he's so soft-spoken that a visitor has to strain to hear him. It's obvious that for Janine Turner, at least, he would lay down his life.

"Yes, sir, I look after Miz Turner, I look after all of them, sir. They're good guys," he says. What could be his concerns in tiny Roslyn?

"Mainly, sir, it's public relations wiv' the people in the streets, sir," he says carefully. "If, for instance, you have to move them along, you have to be careful how you talk them, 'cause it's their town and you have to understand their feelings."

Despite his twenty-seven years of security work experience, mostly in the employ of the wealthy and powerful of the business world, the *Northern Exposure* people are the first celebrities he's ever worked with, and it's clear he adores them. What's the difference?

He smiles shyly. "The people who I worked wiv' didn't want anybody to know what I was, so I could blend in. Therefore, they didn't want publicity." The Englishman pauses to consider.

"Therefore, I've learned a lot in my trade [here]." But, if someone, a fan, is insistent and intrusive?

"I just try and apologize all the time, sir…. In the end you're not warning them and you're not telling them. You don't want them to feel like you're pushing them."

The next day, in Roslyn, when—between takes—Janine Turner happily wades into crowds of her fans, there's ample occasion to watch him practice his subtle art. The fans, of course, remain oblivious to the martial-arts master in their midst.

Later, when Rob Thompson strides into view, White beams approvingly and whispers, "He's mustard."

Huh? "Mustard," as in the yellow stuff?

"Mustard, it mean's he's good," the former Londoner explains, elongating the last word's vowels, "good at his job. It means he's hot."

THE GUEST STAR

Anthony Edwards, heretofore perhaps best known for his role in *Top Gun*, among the seventeen movies he's acted in, is a tall mild-mannered actor with a diffident half-smile, who's signed on for at least seven episodes in the new season to play environmentally battered ex-attorney, Mike Monroe, Cicely's latest resident. His tentative, outside-the-Bubble stroll with a *very* intrigued Maggie is Edwards's first filmed scene. What attracted him to the part?

"The writing, the writing's so good, and it's a great character," he says. "It's hard to find a great character, and this show takes big risks."

Edwards clearly is a craft-minded actor. "The best part of acting is finding out who the character is," he says, "and that comes from finding out rhythms—everybody has different rhythms—but it's all coming out of the script."

What is it that intrigues him about Murphy in his isolated dome? "Probably his sense of humor and the way he deals with things," Edwards replies thoughtfully. "He thinks about things all the time….He's very well-educated and his way of battling this [condition] is, 'I'm going to learn *everything* there is about toxic problems in the world.' From that place of knowledge he then has created a way to survive, and in that survival he's found humor, which makes him attractive to Maggie and a foil for Joel."

When a skeptical visitor, familiar with the ways of Hollywood, suggests that, just perhaps, his character has been brought in in case of any more contract disputes—"you know, Joel'd be in a plane crash or something, then suddenly you'd get well?"—Edward's laughs and drolly replies, "They'd have bigger contract disputes with me."

MAIN STREET SOUNDS

The sun's not yet risen over the Cascades when the crew starts setting up for the day's exterior shooting on Roslyn's familiar main street. The schedule includes a scene in which Ruth-Anne says goodbye to her son outside her store, a Chris-in-the Morning in the cramped K-BEAR studio scene and a Dr. Joel-looks-astounded scene, in which he spots Maggie and Mike Murphy, who's outfitted in one of Maurice's old spacesuits to get around town without being affected by environmental toxins, coming down the street.

By the time of the actors' 9:15 A.M. set call, the street all around the Brick, Washington state's oldest tavern, and the Roslyn Cafe, with that famous mural on its wall, is crowded with hundreds of camcorder-toting tourists from all over the map.

It's safe to say that, ever since the little frontier town was officially named on the 10th of August, 1886, by a vice president of the Northern Pacific Coal Company, supposedly in honor of the New York state town his sweetheart came from, there's been nothing like the effect *Northern Exposure* has had on the locals (and that includes the time in the forties when the residents were shocked to discover that a popular local miner named Joe was actually a young woman named Gloria, who had passed as a man in order to work in the coal mines). By now, it seems as if they're all either on the show as extras or are selling *Northern Exposure*-related paraphernalia in the many quaint shops.

"A sort of interesting index of our success," suggests co-executive producer Rob Thompson, "is the number of people we find in Roslyn every time we go up....Because when we started, there was nobody. It was not a ghost town, but it was just this sleepy little mining town in the mountains. And now, if you go on the weekend...it's just packed wall-to-wall."

"It's gone from a sleepy little town to the Universal backlot," is how one crew member puts it.

[Roslynians, of course, would disagree. "It's always been a tourist destination for people who want a weekend getaway from Seattle," sniffs one Roslyn native, although "you can't compare the way it is now with the way it was before the show. Because you know, it's just insane, the way tourism is now."

[This resident also claims that, several years ago, his mother bought a "beautiful house on almost three-quarters of an acre for, I think it was $2,500. And now it's gone through the roof; there are houses on the market here for $150,000."]

Supervising sound mixer Glenn Micallef finds Roslyn "an interesting place in terms of sounds."

He's in charge of sound recording on location and has been with the show since the very beginning. "It's a rural town and has some typical noise problems related to rural towns—noisy mufflers, the Brick Tavern [that] on Fridays [has] a lot of music booming out of it, and it's really windy around here."

Life goes on in picturesque little Roslyn, but in a sense the town has become the show. Totem poles on the man drag and antlers on some walls that the production had put up are now part of the general civic decor. Roslyn, in fact, is evolving into Cicely.

"There's some kind of eerie similarities from some of the characters of the show and some of the residents of Roslyn," a young second-generation Roslyn native later opines. "Like Holling. You know, the owner of the Brick Tavern [is] a man in his mid- to late-fifties, and his girlfriend is, like, somewhere in her late twenties, but she acts like she's sixteen, maybe seventeen....I think they caused a bit of a commotion with their age differences. I mean, she has blond hair, and he—there's definitely physical similarities as well as personality similarities...

"There's a man that lives here in town that's about the same age as Ed," this Roslyn native continues, "I guess in his early- to mid-twenties—leather jacket, black kinda long hair like Ed. He works at the theater, so he has a connection to the movies like Ed does. Same basic physique. And Ruth-Anne's character, I mean, she's pretty comparable to a lot of old ladies who live here in town."

Nah, how many ladies do you know like Ruth-Anne?

"Action!"

"*Action!*"

A big lumber truck rolls through town, oblivious of the needs of the TV show, stopping everything.

"Hold it. Hold it there. Freeze."

Production assistants and young interns in orange safety vests hush the hundreds of tourists watching across the broad, country street and looking in from down the block, moving them politely well away from the shot.

"Roll, please."

"Rolling."

Dr. Joel comes out and stares down the street again.

JANINE AND THE FANS

Between takes, Janine Turner, with John White discreetly by her side, wanders over to a knot of fifty or so curious, excited people—a potpourri of vacationing Americana.

"Hi," she calls out brightly. They surge around her, surrounding her on three sides. The bodyguard stands close by, his arms loosely out, not stiff and not extended, but just enough to create a space for the magnetic young beauty.

"Oh, a *Northern Exposure* calendar." She takes it, seemingly genuinely interested, and the pro-ferred pen and signs the calendar for an excited teenage girl.

"Thank you, ma'am," says Britisher John White. "If you'll just step back."

"Wife and I were here a year ago, decided to come back," declares a man in a polo shirt and madras shorts.

"What do you know. Oh, really?" His wife shyly holds up a camera, as the man steps to Turner's side.

He beams, she smiles brightly, the wife snaps off a shot and White moves him away with a handshake and an approving grin.

"Oooh, look at that picture of me. What a terrible picture!" Turner takes the publicity still from another dewy-eyed young girl's hand. "They sure don't ask me. Where would you like me to sign it? Anywhere?"

"Would you just sign it 'To Mary-Ann'?"

"Mary-Ann? Is that you?"

"Uh-uh." The girl shakes her head shyly. "Somebody else."

"Oh-oh." Turner shakes the pen. "Out of ink."

Several men in the group reach for their pockets all at once, but John White quickly and smoothly slips another pen into the actress' hand.

"When you gonna kill that Fleischman?" one of the men wants to know.

The actress shrieks with delight. "Well, hopefully we won't go that far." She checks with the shy little girl for the correct spelling of the name, signs, and hands the photograph back. The girl is thrilled.

White spots an orange-vested production assistant with a walkie-talkie at the edge of the crowd. He leans in, tells the actress quietly, "They're ready for you again, Miz Turner," then turns to the crowd and says brightly, "Sorry, folks, Miz Turner's wanted."

JOHN AND THE FANS

Actor John (Chris-in-the-Morning) Corbett, finishing his scene at the radio station set (the small red-brick building with green trim is actually a warehouse, and has props stored in the back), lopes over to a group of fans and is immediately surrounded by wide-eyed teenage girls and their equally admiring mothers, pointing cameras and video recorders.

"How ya doin'?" he asks the gathering at large. As he signs autographs and poses for snapshots with the fans, he's all easygoing banter and loose-limbed charm. John White beams approvingly from about twenty feet away.

After about ten minutes of this, Corbett spots Janine Turner heading for one of the minivans. "Hey, guys," he says impishly to the kids around him, "look, it's Janine Turner. Go get her." Then, while they're all looking in her direction, he slips back to the shoot.

REDMOND

In the leafy Seattle suburb of Redmond there is a nondescript industrial park, and in that park is a sprawling featureless warehouse.

Only the topiary bush sculpted into the shape of a moose near the front door suggests that this is the production home and converted soundstage for *Northern Exposure*. Just inside, near where a receptionist answers phones and directs a visitor through a warren of offices and cubicles to the cavernous, dark, and segmented soundstage in back, stands the ten-foot-tall skeleton of Jesse the Bear, now sporting sunglasses and foam-rubber moose antlers. On a table beside Jesse is Maurice Minnifield's antique German clock.

Around the soundstage are the permanent sets, including the interiors of Holling's Bar; Maurice's house and library; the K-BEAR radio station; Ruth-Anne's store; Dr. Joel's cabin, waiting room, exam room and study; and Maggie's house. Dangling from the high ceiling is the fuselage of Maggie's single-engine plane.

Today, the shooting crew is back from Roslyn, and they're on their newest standing set—a second full-sized Dome, built on the soundstage for the sole purpose of filming interiors. On the schedule, are "reverses"—that is, reverse angle shots-of the earlier, Circle 8-location scenes and an inside-the-Dome Maggie-and-Mike scene, in which he convinces her that he's not nuts by identifying her brand of perfume—even though she's just showered and hasn't put any on.

The filming company regularly puts in sixty-hour weeks to meet its production schedule. Every few weeks, say the crew members, that goes up to seventy-two hours per week. It's a killing pace, and the long days are filled with everlasting repetition and endless waits.

FRONT ELEVATION
3" = 1'-0"

BASE PLAN
3" = 1'-0"

NORTHERN EXPOSURE

FOR CBS AT PIPELINE PRODUCTIONS
PRODUCTION DESIGNER: WOODY CROCKER
PLAN FOR: CLOCK
DATE: 6·5·92   SCALE: 3"=1'-0"
DRAWN BY: MARK WOLF

HOLLING'S BAR

The actual Brick in Roslyn is a real tavern, where you can down a brew, shoot some stick and munch on the famous Brick popcorn, which is sprinkled with brewer's yeast; like all bars, it's somewhat sour, gloomy and dark, while Holling's Bar is a bright, magicky show-biz place.

At Holling's, the bathroom doors, which of course lead nowhere, are labeled "guys" and "dolls," with pictures of, respectively, James Dean and Marilyn Monroe (in her famous skirt-swirling, Seven Year Itch pose).

A totem and a moosehead wearing a hard hat are on the wall, along with a scattering of photographs, which turn out to be mostly candid shots of the cast and crew, and posters for such Alaskan exotica as the Iditarod sled dog race, Alaskan vodka, Snow Cap Ale, and a bumpersticker that reads: *In Alaska If You Ain't the Lead Dog, Your View Will Never Change.*

Also on the walls are flags, animals heads, antlers, and a porcelain toilet seat that frames a crude drawing of a freaked-out cartoon face and is labeled *Ralph Porcelain Prince.*

The pool-cue holders on the walls are made from animal hooves and the pinball machine is a Cyclone Mystery Wheel.

Taped to the wall near the small bar (like all sets, it looks much bigger on TV) are guest checks, including one for biscuits and gravy ($4.75), and a real menu from the real Brick.

A salmon-colored piano stands in the corner; the casually spread-out sheet music includes "September Song," arranged for piano and accordion.

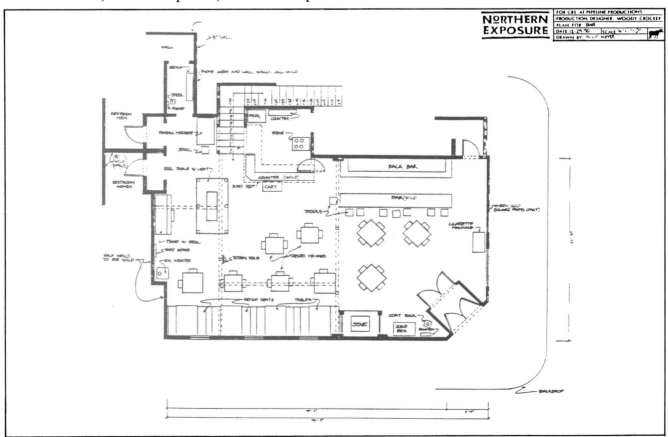

THE PRODUCTION DESIGNER

Woody Crocker, *Northern Exposure's* Emmy-winning production designer (for the episode in which his art department re-created turn-of-the-century Cicely), sits behind a desk crowded with drawings and models and praises his "marvelous, just marvelous" thirty-five-person crew, which is responsible for drafting, set decoration, construction, painting, greenskeeping, and props.

They've just finished the most expensive of the eighty-some standing sets they've built for the show—the two domes, which together cost approximately $100,000.

"You could've built a [real] house," Crocker says, jokingly inviting his visitor to "come and move in. We can use the rent money."

Frontier Cicely was constructed for about $80,000, he says, or about $15,000 over budget. "Generally, what they do ask [from us] is impossible, in the time frame anyway," he says with a chuckle.

Among his favorites creations: the medieval clock, Jesse the Bear, the Napoleonic soldier encased in ice, the Indian costumes and decorations for the Raven Dancers, and, of course, the trebuchet.

Sometimes, he adds details to a set that the home viewer can't possibly see: "In Holling's apartment, in his bedroom and his living room, all the artwork—and we have tons of it—is paint-by-numbers. We figure that Holling, in his lonely nights before he met Shelly, would sit and paint by numbers.

"Now, he only has a couple of unfinished ones," Crocker adds with a chuckle, "because, since he met Shelly, he doesn't have time for paint-by-numbers or any other kind of painting.

"I'm hoping they'll write an episode where Holling will have a one-man show and it will have to be judged or attended by Joel. And he will be incensed that they are all paint-by-numbers, but the rest of the town thinks it's perfectly normal."

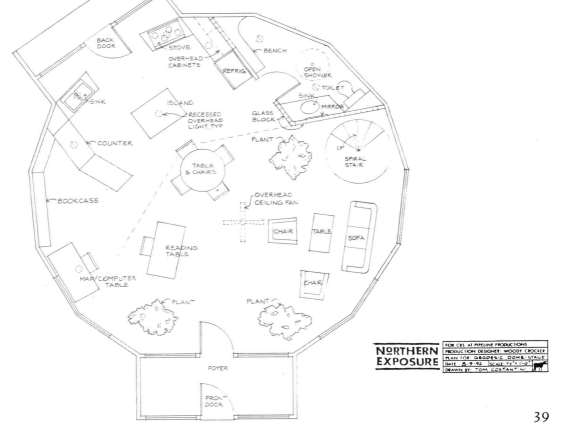

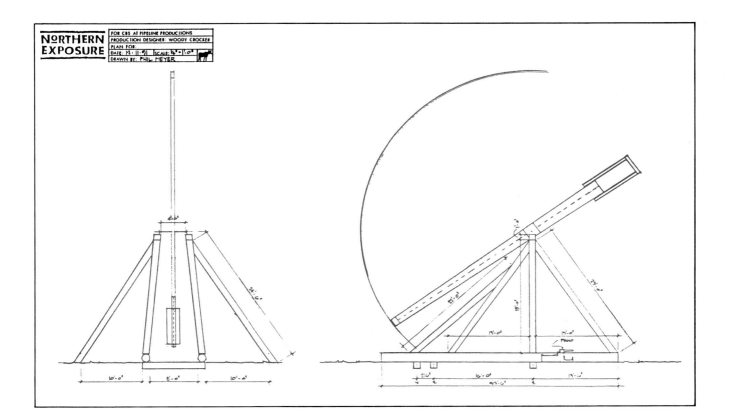

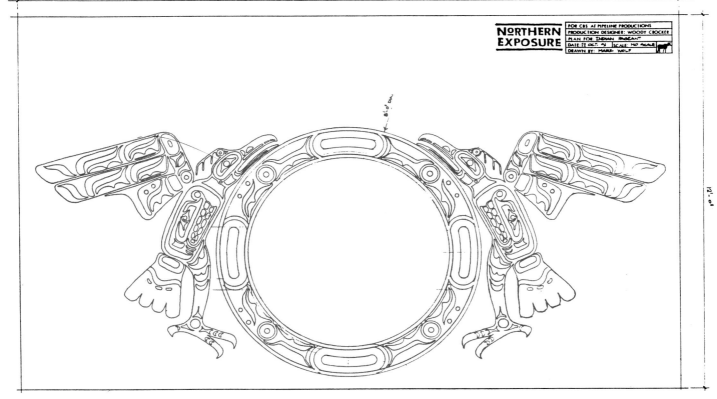

CUT OUT
THIS EDGE
ONLY

CUT OUT
THIS EDGE
ONLY

12'-0"

12'-0"

4'-0"

4'-0"

NORTHERN EXPOSURE

FOR CBS AT PIPELINE PRODUCTIONS	
PRODUCTION DESIGNER: WOODY CROCKER	
PLAN FOR: INDIAN PAGEANT	
DATE: 23 OCT. 91	SCALE: 1" = 1'-0"
DRAWN BY: MARK WOLF	

ROB MORROW INTERVIEWED

He's not on call today, but actor Rob Morrow shows up at the Holling's Bar set anyway to do a TV-news interview. He's wearing black sandals, baggy green shorts, a black MTV tee-shirt, and has a blue-and-white bandanna tied on his head.

Morrow takes a seat at the bar stool, clips on a tiny microphone and the interview begins. His interviewer is a professionally peppy female field producer for a nationally known show.

Are you happy to have all the controversy surrounding you behind you now?

Yeah. Absolutely.

How are things on the set?

Great.... I know those people pretty well, and there was no tension as a result of what was going on with me.

People benefitted, if anything.

What do you think of the new character added this season?

It's very smart to inject new life... it's been done successfully with other shows.

If they can sustain the inevitable with Maggie and Joel by injecting some new element that will take it off on a tangent for a while without having to continue to bait back and forth... I think it's very smart. And personally, it's great to bring in new actors, especially someone like Tony Edwards who I really like... It breaks the monotony.

Does it help to keep Dr. Fleischman fresh?

Yeah. Anything that makes me continue to work and look and change. A new element makes me look at how to incorporate that into what I'm doing, it keeps me from being complacent.

Part of the attraction of the show to a lot of people is the sexual tension between Joel and Maggie. How far can you keep that up?

I don't know. I think that they just bought themselves a lot of time in a way that won't be a problem with this other character. If something happens between the two of them... that's a perfect way to kind of put us off.... Eventually, it's going to happen, it will come to a head, so to speak.

How far do you think you can go in this show with explicit sexual scenes?

I don't know what the standards in television are for that...

How comfortable are you?

I'm cool with it. I have no real hang-ups about doing stuff. I don't like doing things for exploitive reasons, if it were just to do something. But I'm the kind of person, if the scene were about someone doing it right there, I would have no problems about getting as close to that approximation as possible. I like that, that's fun for me, to go to the limit.

Would you be in favor of something more happening on the show with your character and other women, or with Maggie?

Sure... Again, any new element that's put in the show will break the monotony for me. And being how I like women so much, it wouldn't be bad [chuckle].

You know, nobody ever describes the show as monotonous, but I know what you're saying. But really, the fans expect some-

thing so weird everytime they tune into the show...

Right, right. I'm not saying the show is monotonous, that the stories are monotonous. I'm saying that as an actor, doing a TV series can be monotonous.

I have to kick myself really hard to continue to work, because you find yourself in the same scenes, on the same sets with the same actors, basically, and...every once in a while I'll go home after a long week and say, "Can I just phone that in?" So, that's what I mean about the monotony...

You started to talk about this new character, and his relationship with Maggie. What can we expect from his introduction?

I don't know. They're toying with a kind of attraction. I haven't read down the line...

Can you tell us a little about this guy Monroe, and Fleischman's interaction with him?

Basically, he chose Cicely because it's the least polluted spot in the U.S....He's someone who can't be exposed to the atmosphere, to any kind of artificial chemicals or synthetic fabrics. So he's built this dome in outer Cicely. And as a citizen, I'm obligated to take care of him...

Now that all this contract stuff is behind you, can you talk to me about how it feels to be back at work, with the producers and everybody else? How are the relationships?

I was never *away* from work...So that's one thing, I never missed a day of work. And, what was going on with me had nothing to do with the creatives and the production team.

I'm actually feeling really good this year. It's odd, I thought that, maybe as time would go on, I would get more bored, but I kind of found a way this year to reinvest. I'm enjoying the work.

Can you give us any insight into what makes Joel so attracted to Maggie, but it's sort of a love-hate relationship?

I think, well, purely on a physical level it's very obvious why I'd be attracted to her. On an emotional level, I think he respects her strength, and her independence, and her passion. Those are characteristics that he admires in people, and to have them be matched with someone who's attractive. Unfortunately, so many of the ideas she has are diametrically opposed to his, but nevertheless she is committed to them.

When someone is very strong and clear about something, whether they are right or wrong, it's always interesting.

You said you enjoyed coming back this year, and that you've found a way to rejuvenate yourself, and motivate your-self....What have you done?

I'm just kind of working a little harder. I started to get into this thing where I felt like I was just memorizing lines, and it just started to scare me. I thought, Oh boy, here we go, it's over, it's gone. So it's taking a lot more time at night, I'm kind of rehearsing by myself a lot. It's just kind of rekindled that desire to act...And the nature of television doesn't allow for that, so I'm making it on my own time.

Has the success of the show changed your life at all?

Yeah. People will talk to me, people are nice to me. It's great, you know, I go to the restaurant and get a table...It's great, because whenever I'm some place by myself, I can always have a conversation because somebody always wants to talk to me, so that's nice.

THE WRITERS

If Diane Frolov and Andrew Schneider, *Northern Exposure's* Emmy-winning husband-and-wife writing team, moved in next door to, say, Adam and Eve, they'd seem right at home in colorful Cicely.

After all, she used to go to Berkeley, where she majored in theology and dance; he was there, too, studying Russian literature. But although their paths kept almost crossing, they didn't meet until years later, when they were both writers down in L.A. So, how did they finally meet?

"Our agent introduced us," they say simultaneously, both breaking into laughter.

Hardest to write, they agree, are the Chris-in-the-Morning speeches.

"That's the really tough one," says she. "You have to do a lot of research...[and] you have to think of it in terms of theme."

"If [Chris] has three or four speeches throughout an episode," he adds, "very often they are connected and they're one piece."

Although their working style is to "literally sit down together and write every scene and every page and every line together," as he puts it, they do have their specialities.

"She's the theologian," says he. "I do sex and she does death."

"I'm definitely death," she agrees blithely.

"She's death and god," he amplifies. "I'm, like, banana peels."

What do they like best about writing for the show? "The ability to be intelligent and get away with it," he says, while she nods solemn agreement. "We were encouraged to write 'up' whenever we could."

Jed

NORTHERN EXPOSURE
"Blowing Bubbles"

Pipeline Productions
ONELINE SCHEDULE

Shoot Day #1 -- Tue, Aug 11, 1992

INT Joel's Ofc./Exam Rm.   DAY
     Maggie delivers medical items, Joel tells about Mike Monroe

Scs. 12,13
Story Day 1

INT Waiting Room   DAY
     Joel admonishes Maggie for visiting Mike

Scs. 22
Story Day 2

INT Waiting Room   DAY
     Joel figures out Maggie's attraction to Mike   End Day #1

Scs. 28pt.
Story Day 3

Shoot Day #2 -- Wed, Aug 12, 1992

INT Ruth-Anne's Store   DAY
     Matthew tells why he came

Scs. 11
Story Day 1

INT Ruth-Anne's Store   DAY
     Matthew talks about tackle shop idea

Scs. 21
Story Day 2

INT Maurice's Office   DAY
     Ruth-Anne tells Maurice to stay out of her family business

Scs. 26
Story Day 3

INT Radio Station   End Day #2
     Chris regarding Mike and Proust

Scs. 29
Story Day 3

-- Thu, Aug 13, 1992   DAY
                                              Matthew, Joel and Maggie go around re Mike

INT Bar   DAY
     Ruth-Anne wonders about Matthew
                                              ...ed about his idea   End Day #3

46

THE PRODUCTION ASSISTANT (P.A.)

"Hi, my name is Deven Fredericks, and I'm a production assistant in the office. I started on the set—I've been with the show since the beginning, the very beginning—I was an intern.

"And I'd just like to say that this show has more creative input than any show I've ever been on. It started like a baby; it developed into something *incredible*. It was, like, a show they thought would never make it.

"We all started, everybody was new, we didn't know what was ahead of us, and we all became united. It was the most *friendliest*, you know, *compassionate* production that turned into something, you know, more than anyone ever expected."

After eight days of shooting, the episode wraps. Early the following morning the next shoot begins.

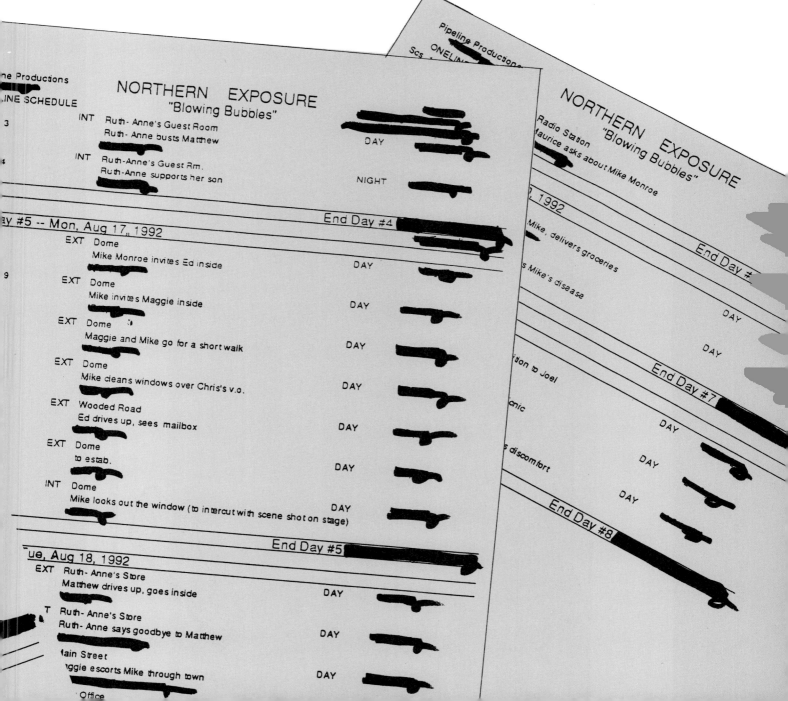

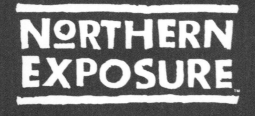

THE CREATORS

Nearly ten percent of *all* nominations at the 1992 nighttime Emmy Awards went to shows created by just one producing team—Brand-Falsey.

Joshua Brand and John Falsey, now both fortysomething baby boomers, are also both onetime students of literature (Brand has a masters in English Lit from Columbia, and Falsey, who once sold a short story to the *New Yorker*, was a resident at the Iowa Writers School), who met in the late seventies in a Hollywood screening room. Both were up individually for episode-writing jobs on a new series from MTM Productions, the television production company founded by Grant Tinker and Mary Tyler Moore.

"We were watching a pilot for a television show called *The White Shadow*," Brand recalls. "I had never been in a room before watching a pilot and neither had he. We didn't know if we were supposed to talk to each other or not, take notes or not take notes. Anyway, we started to talk together and afterwards we went out and had a cup of coffee at the Winchell's Donuts across the street."

Falsey got the job, and sometime later Brand, who then was making ends meet working as a grip, got the boot. Fortunately, that's when he got a call from Falsey: "He said, 'They've just made me a story editor. Would you like to write a script of *The White Shadow*?' He had never read anything of mine, we had just sort of met each other twice, and I jumped at the opportunity."

Eventually, after that series was cancelled, Brand got to return the favor. He had sold MTM on the idea of an ensemble series set in a teaching hospital—"*Hill Street Blues* in a hospital"—and he brought Falsey in as his partner to cocreate the show, which became the highly acclaimed *St. Elsewhere*.

Nearly a decade-and-a-half later, as all those Emmy nominations (and *Northern Exposure*'s sub-sequent win as Outstanding Drama Series in 1992) demonstrated, they are the epitome of Hollywood's hot writer-producers.

Theirs is a high-wire balancing act—an endless round of network and story meetings, of writing and rewriting, of casting, scoring, and editing.

When they work together, as they did on the *Northern Exposure* pilot, "you just really thrash things out, [so that] both partners are...making the same product," says Brand, "seeing the same characters, seeing them the same way, finding the same voice for the characters.

"We pretty much feel that we, initially, have to sit in a room together and just hammer it out. Once the show gets going, like in all of our shows, then in fact we pretty much just separate, and John will take one script and I'll take another, and [we'll] stay out of each other's hair."

At the time they sat down to talk with a visitor to their Santa Monica offices one hazy, late-summer day, Brand and Falsey were juggling three one-hour weekly series. One on each of the Big Three networks.

The strain didn't show. Like most everyone else at their production company's offices, they dressed down (jeans and running shoes seemed de rigueur) and were laid back.

After all those years of working together, they still seemed genuinely to like each other.

The three series they were then shepherding through fall-season '92 premieres all were adult shows written for adults and they all shared the Brand-Falsey trademarks—offbeat, fully realized characters, witty scripts, and on-location shoots (Atlanta for NBC's *I'll Fly Away*, Jamaica for ABC's *Going to Extremes*, and bewitching little Roslyn, Washington, for CBS's *Northern Exposure*).

How did the idea for **Northern Exposure** *come about?*

JOSH: Part of our job is to come up with ideas for television shows. It *is* our job.

My friend Lance, who's my oldest friend, subsequently became—after becoming a doctor [first]—a New York City policeman, and, after that, moved to upstate New York, [to] a rural community, to practice medicine. Part of the genesis of it was from my friend Lance, part of it was from some movies: *Never Cry Wolf, Local Hero, Amarcord.*

We sort of evolved this idea of this doctor, who we initially thought would be in the bayous of Louisiana, but who we ultimately felt should be in Alaska....As the last frontier, it gave us a greater contrast. So I think that was the genesis of the idea to begin with.

You know, there is a book of fellowships that you can apply for in anything, and although we didn't know or think that the state of Alaska offered a medical fellowship, we knew that there were all kinds of fellowships for all kinds of things.

It didn't seem that we took dramatic license to think...that this state, that really wasn't getting needed doctors, offers a scholarship. And, after the fact, we did find out that there were incidents that were, if not the same, similar.

You came up with the basic idea, then what happened? How did you go from there to the characters?

JOSH: Before we pitched it to the network, the studio [Universal] came to us and said, "The network's interested in doing this idea for a summer series, would you guys be interested in doing it?" And we said yes.

I guess that was in January or February of '89, and we had to shoot it in April, in order to get it on the air in the summer.

So we just sat down and knocked out some

characters and started thrashing it out.

JOHN: The character evolvement is just the normal process of really locking yourself in a room for four hours a day and slowly forming a character. We start with a Maurice, or with an Ed; and Josh comes up with part of his character, I come up with part of his character, until we feel comfortable enough that we have a fully formed human being.

I've read, I think, every script, and I'm surprised by how fully formed the characters were from the pilot script on. I mean, they have evolved, but...

JOHN: Peter Tortorici, who is the senior vice president at CBS, saw the pilot fairly recently, and he was surprised at just how well it held up. The characters have evolved, but they essentially have remained the same.

Is that unusual for you? Was it like that on your other shows?

JOSH: I think to a large extent it was. That's the thing I think we do best, write characters. But that's one of the things I'm particularly proud of with *Northern Exposure*—the characters are so fully formed.

I think generally we write good characters, so I don't know if it is significantly different, but I think it may be a little different.

I imagine you had Joel first. What was the next character?

JOHN: Honestly, we'd be guessing. We certainly wanted someone who represented the best and the worst of Alaska, who became Maurice Minnifield, the man who saw Alaska for its beauty, but also for its potential—its expansion, its tourism and that sort of thing. And then we went on to Ed, and to Marilyn and so on.

Josh was especially key to the Holling-Shelly,

May-December romance. I remember that coming up and he was especially keen on that part...But that was three years ago, I don't remember much more.

JOSH: I don't remember it exactly the same way John does—it's our own *Rashomon*—but from my way of thinking that was Chaucer's *Miller's Tale*.

The old miller with the young wife—that is as classic a paradigm in literature [as] you get, that goes back to Boccaccio, back hundreds of years. So it wasn't particularly an original idea.

The part that was a little different was when we made it a triangle, with Maurice and Holling and Shelly.

Did you have the relationship first or the triangle?

JOHN: I think we had the triangle first. We had decided that Maurice had brought her up, she was Miss Northwest Passage, because we had that whole thing come out in the pilot.

And you even have a reference in the pilot that the town was founded by lesbians.

JOSH: Yeah. We were up there shooting the pilot and the town was called Cicely—John picked that name out—and there was this big Roslyn Cafe sign...

As we were shooting, the camera would sometimes pick up this sign, and we were thinking, What would this mean in a town called Cicely?

I was standing there and I said, "Well let's put an apostrophe 'S' up there, and say that the town was founded by Roslyn and Cicely, who were these two lesbian lovers..."

JOHN: I believe it was Maurice who explained it. He drove in and explained it to Fleischman, and he says, "But don't believe the rumors."

What about Cicely, how did you come up with that name?

JOHN: We had a very boring name [originally], and I thought I wanted something a little more charming, and I came in one morning and said, "What do you think of the name Cicely?"

And Josh thought it was like Sicily, Italy, and I said, "No, like the woman's name. Like [actress] Cicely Tyson." And he said, "Oh yeah, that's pretty."

The characters on the page sound like the people who play them, but the pilot was written before it was cast. How did you find these people?

JOSH: To make a good anything, it's script, casting and location.

We generally prefer working with actors who are not associated with a particular role. In this instance, it was not only something we would *prefer* to do, but we had to do because it was a summer replacement.

We didn't have a whole lot of money. We knew we were going to be using actors that were not as well known. Obviously, John Cullum [Holling] is a Broadway star and was known to us because of that. Barry Corbin [Maurice] was somebody who was a well-known character actor, but nobody knew his name. But the other people were people who really hadn't done anything significant in terms of television or movies.

JOHN: In New York, after two or three days of really intense casting sessions, where they bring in hundreds and hundreds of people, Josh and I both felt when Rob came in that he was pretty much the one [to play Dr. Joel]...Josh felt very strongly about John Cullum, and I think those were the only two to come out of New York.

We saw a tape of Janine Turner [Maggie O'Connell] sent to us from New York. She was

the last character to be cast, and she came out and did a great reading for the network, so we hired her. The rest of them were cast here in L.A.

What did you see in Rob that was Joel?

JOHN: We didn't really want to cast a Woody Allen type guy. We didn't want to cast the nebbishy guy. The thing about Rob is he's a handsome guy.

JOSH: And he's nobody's schmuck.

JOHN: He's not sort of the nerdy guy with the pencil in his pocket. We consciously didn't want to do that, the "Oh, hey, look it's Woody Allen" bit. So that was something that appealed to us, and he was likable and attractive, and there was some charm to him.

JOSH: There was a little bit of an impish quality about him that we thought would fit in perfectly in the Final Frontier. The classic urban dweller— he's not this big huge strapping guy.

The scene I will always remember from the pilot is when he walks outside at the opening of the third act, and he sees where he is. The cut is him coming over, running...and you know he hasn't run seven miles since the seventh grade. He ran all the way in.

I just remember that picture, and he really was exactly the way I had envisioned him personally...

How about John Corbett, Chris-in-the-Morning, how did you find him?

JOSH: He just came in to read one day. John is also a very charming, likable, ingenuous, genuine person. Although he is a very handsome guy, there isn't a whole lot of narcissism immediately present.

It isn't like he is so totally conscious that he is a really good-looking guy; it's almost effortless with him. We didn't have a specific type in mind for that role, but he was just a very winning, appealing person when he came in.

JOHN: There was one other very strong contender for the part that Josh and I felt good about, [but] the network felt very strongly about John.

We like John and obviously he has been a breakout character, but there was one other actor that I think could have done it. He didn't have the look that John did, but he had certainly the acting ability.

Is it true that you found Cynthia Geary waiting tables?

JOHN: Cynthia was waiting tables at the time. She told me that one time when I was up there [in Roslyn]. But we didn't [personally] walk into a restaurant and find her.

You cast it, you shot the pilot, and then some characters that weren't regulars began to catch your eye?

JOSH: We always viewed it as an ensemble piece, to be honest. If you look at the first eight scripts, we pretty much had all the characters in. It wasn't the Joel Fleischman show; it wasn't so much the Joel-Maggie show, although that was pushed.

We had Chris-in-the-Morning, we had Maurice, we had the Shelly-Holling thing going, we had Ed.

So from the beginning we were conscious that we had a whole bunch of really good characters here, so let's not waste them.

It wasn't really a slow evolvement toward ensemble as some shows might be.

How about the town? Any other candidates besides Roslyn?

JOSH: No, there really weren't. We went on a location scout. We saw a number of towns close to Seattle, but they weren't really working out for us. Our production designer at the time...said we ought to take a look at this town called Roslyn—

it was about forty miles away from where we were at the time. I think we were at the Snoqualmie Inn...

It wasn't on our schedule for places to see. We had scouted the Seattle area and the Denver area and the minute we drove into Roslyn, we thought, this is it.

JOHN: You're surrounded by fir trees. I can't tell you the relief we felt when we climbed out of that van and looked around! You couldn't have asked for anything that was better.

I've heard, from letters that I've gotten from native Alaskans, [that] normally the roads of that size aren't paved like they are in Roslyn, and they haven't got above-ground telephone wires. Other than that, it's pretty damn close.

At the beginning, I imagine, you were on the show all the time. Now how does it work?

JOHN: Last year [1991-92], Josh really ran *Northern Exposure*, and I ran *I'll Fly Away*. This year, we're both running *Going to Extremes*, Josh is still overseeing *Northern Exposure*, and although I keep my hand in the pie with *I'll Fly Away*, David Chase is running it day by day.

Do you have a favorite moment, a favorite episode on the show?

JOHN: My favorite episodes of the show [were] *Spring Break* [featuring Cicely's annual Running of the Bulls], and the one where Holling was going to get circumsized. Those are my favorite episodes. I could watch those eighteen times in a row. They are extraordinary shows.

JOSH: I have a bunch of favorites... A moment that I really love is the first time we flung the piano. I thought that was a really cool thing, because building that trebuchet [a medieval catapult] was such a major enterprise. What the art department does on the show is just extraordinary.

I assume that the biggest expense per episode is the actors' salaries. Would you rank it for me?

JOSH [laughs]: I think it's probably John's salary that's the biggest.

JOHN: I think it's probably ours. To be honest with you, the salaries were all pretty low to begin with; they are rising now. I don't think the show is an overly expensive one.

JOSH: The show isn't. All the shows that we've done are in the low to mid-range in terms of the cost of one-hour shows. Even now, this is not one of the more expensive shows in television. It's not the cheapest now; it's a hit show, so it generates a lot of income.

JOHN: It would help if he wouldn't keep taking his director's residual every week.

JOSH: I don't get a director's residual on that. I get it on *I'll Fly Away*.

JOHN [laughs]: We need the money, Josh, give it back.

How about the cost of licensing music and of production design?

JOSH: Music licensing on this show in particular is very expensive. We use a lot of music, especially a lot of source music [*i.e., music coming from a particular "source" in a scene, such as a jukebox or a radio*].

We spend a significant amount—not as much as, I'm sure, a show like *Miami Vice* did, or other shows that used hit songs.

We *don't* use hit songs, we try to shy away from them, but we do use a lot of source music, so we spend more money on this show on music than on any other show [of ours].

JOHN: You know, *I'll Fly Away* doesn't spend anything, mainly because we can take any type of old 1950s song as source and pick it up for $400.

On an average episode, if there is such a thing, is the second biggest expense the music licensing, and then the production?

JOSH: No, you would have to break it down. But your above-the-line costs, your writers, your actors, your directors, your producers, those are lumped together as your above-the-line costs, those are the biggest expense.

Once you get into your below-the-line-cost, your building, production, on this show it's very expensive, because we build a lot on every episode.

Building something like a trebuchet, the Bubble Man's house, or any of the other things that we continue to build, *is really* expensive. Music is very expensive, but relative to the over-all pattern of the show, it's not that significant.

What was the hardest episode to do?

JOHN: You've really got to go to the pilot.
JOSH: The pilot was really the hardest.
JOHN: Let me tell, let me tell. This guy [i.e., Josh] did an heroic job. First of all, we had no money. I think we shot it for $839,000; it was a joke.

I think he shot it in eleven days, something like that, twelve days. We had a crew that was so inexperienced that you couldn't even do a tilt-up [i.e., the camera move] correctly.

And what he went through, and the embarrassment I can only imagine Josh must have felt looking at some of those dailies—when you have second A.D.s [assistant directors] who don't know how to move extras around—was extraordinary!

As you see, what he was able to accomplish under really, really, *really* difficult situations—I mean this crew didn't know what it was doing. And changes were made, I think made by the third episode, no by the second episode, but this guy...

I must tell you. The first day we were shooting, I was there for the first half of it...
JOSH: The trucks didn't arrive...
JOHN: The trucks didn't arrive for two-and-a-half hours!
JOSH: And then they had to move the crane, they brought the wrong crane...
JOHN: But I remember, one guy couldn't do the tilt-up to even get the fact that it was Fairbanks airport or something like that...It was a nightmare.

I walked over and got [Josh] a beer, it was extraordinary. The film was great, but it was just really, really difficult.

Do you have the same essential crew?

JOSH: No, no, not at all. The crew is a fabulous crew, and has been for a very long time. They are great.

It's what, about one-hundred-thirty people?

JOHN: Somewhere between one-hundred, one-hundred-fifty, somewhere around there.
JOSH: But no, the crew that we dealt with on the pilot was replaced, a lot of the most problematic positions were replaced in the next episode.

They didn't want to replace them when I was shooting, because they thought it was because of me.

We have had a number of shows that we, in our opinion, have had to manufacture in post-production. It's a really hard show to groove, because built into the groove is sort of the element of freshness and spontaneity, and how do you groove *that* into a show? And if it does get grooved into a show, then it can't be what it sets out to be. It becomes a little self-conscious.

What's the biggest danger with this show?

JOSH: The danger is that it loses its, well, it's a

little bit like a soufflé when it works. It's lighter than air and yet it has some substance to it. It's when it gets a little too heavy and it doesn't feel particularly fresh, then it isn't quite as interesting.

JOHN: I'm truly of the belief—and believe me I'm a major fan of *I'll Fly Away*; we both cocreated both shows—but I really believe in my heart...that *Northern Exposure* is the second-best hour television in the history of television. Second only to *Hill Street*.

It is so innovative and so creative, and so inspired, and smart. It's unlike any show that's ever been on television before.

And yet, can you articulate what the elements are that make it that way? What is it about the show?

JOHN: I think it is the sense of a non-judgmental universe, the sense of an extended family...

Our personal families are scattered all over the country—my brother's here, grandparents are there—there's a sense of extended family, a non-judgmental family.

It's like opening up a window and getting a breath of fresh air. People want to live in Cicely. People want to know the people in Cicely, they want them to be their friends. And I think the magic qualities that happen—whether it's the aurora borealis, or the spring break that makes everybody a little crazy, and Holling's fighting Sergeant Semanski [the female state trooper], and then everything cracked and it's okay.

It is such an incredibly innovative and imaginative show. I think that's what it is. Once that innovativeness and imagination are lost, and the ideas drop a notch, that's when I think the show will suffer.

And so far through thirty-eight plus—what, twelve scripts just this year?—through fifty, it hasn't happened yet, and that's quite a feat.

What are the big issues coming up for Cicely? Will the moment come when Joel and Maggie finally make it?

JOSH: What people consider the big moments, we don't necessarily consider to be the big moments. Honestly, I know people come up to me and say, "Is Joel going to nail Maggie?"

JOHN: That does seem to be the big question that the audience does have, Are they finally going to do it?

And what's the answer?

JOSH: The answer is, yes and no. The real answer is, that that isn't something that is of great concern to us...

We don't feel that we're *not* doing it because we're trying to avoid something. We feel that we're not doing it because it's far more interesting to us not to do it then to do it.

JOHN: Yeah, it keeps the tension up. And also quite frankly, you've got this wealth of other characters to mine. And to delve into their stories. It's something that's always there: will we or won't we? At some point, will it happen? [*Editor's Note:* In true TV fashion, just in time for the February 1993 sweeps, it did.]

Who thought of making Chris such a philosopher?

JOHN: That was really Josh. I'll have to give that to Josh.

JOSH: Well, I don't really remember. But what was interesting about the character to me was that he is a true intellectual—not an academic, but somebody to whom ideas are real. He's an ex-juvenile delinquent, and he's been in the pen, and the combination of those elements seems to be very fun and very fresh.

JOHN: I think what was most interesting about him, I remember we were sitting around one

Sunday...and the character of Chris had been written, and we were rewriting him—he appeared in the second episode—and we had both agreed that we liked the idea that he was a juvenile delinquent, and he probably spent time in prison. We found that funny.

The twist, which really was Josh, was...as he broke into a house, as he was rifling through some drawer, taking some woman's jewelry, he came across the book that changed his life. I think it was the Whitman...

JOSH: It was *Leaves of Grass*...

JOHN: And when Josh said that, I broke up

laughing, and right there was the character. An intellectual ex-con...

How about making Maurice an ex-astronaut, whose idea was that?

JOSH: Well, that was John's idea.

JOHN: I had been looking at the movie, *The Right Stuff*. And I just saw these guys.

I didn't see any of the particular guys as Maurice, but the idea of an astronaut—patriotic, tough—appealed to me.

I said, "Josh, Maurice has got to be an ex-astronaut." And he goes, "Alright, alright." And

I was so excited about it, [but] he says, "That's been done before." And I said, "When?"

And he said, "Jack Nicholson in *Terms of Endearment*."

JOSH: The thing about the character of Maurice is, we both wanted him to represent what was best and worst about being an American. And the thing about an astronaut is, it's in a sense the contemporary cowboy, and it was a variation on that...That's the cowboy.

Who came up with Adam, this crackpot gourmet?

JOHN: The Adam character was originally a character I had come up with. I wanted someone who had been an ex-Vietnam guy who was out there in the woods....I wanted to write the character seriously, as a serious guy who was disturbed.

And Josh's feeling was...we have to have a twist on it, and the twist is he has to be the cowardly lion...a pathological liar....Then the idea of making Eve this super-hypochondriac went really hand-in-hand with making him a pathological liar.

What about Bernard?

JOSH: We talked about Chris's brother showing up and I said, "Well you know, what if he's black?" and you [John] looked at me and sort of checked, like, "What is he, high or something?"

I was thinking a little bit like in Shakespeare's *As You Like It*. People being related. There's a way that they can be related and sort of integrated to get into the show.

JOHN: Absolutely. As a matter of fact, that's another example of the magicalness of the show...

JOSH: John uses the word magic, and it certainly is in the show, but I think that that's [only] true for some episodes. But what's *always* true is the charm...

JOHN: As Gary Goldberg [a TV writer-producer] said, it's oddly believable.

Quirky is the word everybody always uses about the show.

JOSH: Some people call it quirky....If we all behave *not* according to other people's expectations of how we should behave, we would all inevitably be quirky.

JOHN: I think also the world, certainly the Lower Forty-Eight, has become so sped up and so complicated—the drive to succeed and the rising costs of living, the traffic problems, the smog problems—I think it raises everybody's blood pressure. It's just a fact.

And to be able to turn on the television set and look at this town that has fresh air, and that doesn't have to worry about locking your doors at night, where people are friendly....I think that's very, very appealing to people.

THE REGULARS

From the beginning, say John Falsey and Josh Brand, the show's creators, *Northern Exposure* was never intended to be just the Dr. Joel Show, or even the Joel 'n' Maggie Show.

The play, and the ensemble players, were always *the* things.

In Brand and Falsey's pilot episode there were seven "regulars"—Joel Fleischman, Maggie O'Connell, Maurice Minnifield, Holling Vincoeur, and three characters who, at that time, had only first names: Shelly, Chris and Ed.

Marilyn and Ruth-Anne, at that point, were just part of the "guest" cast.

Even in the pilot episode, written before the show was cast, the characters and their conflicts are sharply drawn. But Falsey, Brand, and the other writers also wrote to the characters, and the actors, who "worked." That's how Peg Phillips (Ruth-Anne) and Elaine Miles (Marilyn) earned their change in status to series regulars after the first, abbreviated, eight-episode summer season.

Oftentimes, as the series continued—quickly moving from summer replacement to cult hit to one of the most popular and most honored hour shows in TV—the writers wove their fictional plots with elements of the various actors' own public personalities, in what amounted to a never-ending feedback loop. "Quirkiness," "whimsy," "charm"…yes, just as the critics said; but there always was that eerie echo. Just as real life and TV lives leaked into each other on *Roseanne* and *Murphy Brown*, Cicely, and its colorful denizens, became more real than Roslyn, Washington, the actual little town where the show films.

If the tabloids discover veteran character actor Barry Corbin's "love child," *Northern Exposure*'s husband-and-wife writing team of Diane Frolov and Andrew Schneider write a script ("Seoul Mates") in which his character, ex-astronaut Maurice Minnifield, has to come to terms with his own grown half-Korean son, fathered when Maurice had been a young, wartime pilot. And they got the writing Emmy for it, too.

If actor John Corbett quickly becomes a heartthrob and a magazine-cover sex symbol, then deejay Chris Stevens, who was barely a presence in the pilot, is soon discovered to have the Stevens Family Pheremones, glandular secretions that periodically make him irresistible to Cicely's women.

And sometimes, surreally, the feedback loop seems to go in the other direction, too. Is there some cosmic connection between the fact that Joel Fleischman, M.D., is desperate to get out of his contract with the State of Alaska to provide medical services to the tiny hamlet of Cicely and the fact that actor Rob Morrow had a highly publicized row with the studio over the terms of his own contract? It's a question for Chris-in-the-Morning, at the very least, but of one thing you can be sure: both Joel and Rob are sensitive, intelligent, highly strung guys, with a well-developed sense of put-upon morality.

"The writers pick up on the predilections, and the talents and the interests of our people in a kind of almost prescient way," is how co-executive producer (and director) Rob Thompson puts it. "They really nail things. We get scripts back that are almost telepathic in the way that the writers are able to interpret…things that are going on within our actors' lives and put them up on the screen…

"As the season progressed last year, and as the season progresses this year, almost all of our actors came up at one point or another and said, 'You know, this is really amazing, but here they are doing this in script eight or twenty-two, and this is something that is happening in my own life.'"

One of the things that was happening to these actors—whether veterans, like Barry Corbin and John Cullum, or former struggling unknowns, like Cynthia Geary and John Corbett—at faster-than-light media-mania speed is…

Fame, and the kind of universal, intoxicating celebrity that only a hit TV series can bring.

Tabloid-fever!…Nosy hacks sniffing around for scandal!…Contract renegotiations!…Lucrative commercial deals!…Unrelenting professional obligations!…Personal traumas!…Conflicting Demands!…Murky opportunities!…Autograph hounds, Groupies and the General Public in all its Frenzied Glory!…

In the midst of this, on the eve of the Emmys and under accelerating pressures of a new fall season, every one of the show's regulars eventually took time out to talk to a visitor—either on location, on the set or, in one case, by phone the morning of the Emmys.

ROB MORROW

(JOEL FLEISCHMAN, MD)

As Josh Brand, the show's co-creator says, Rob Morrow is "nobody's schmuck." What he is is a committed actor, whose first breaks came on the New York stage. Before *Northern Exposure*, there were more than thirty-five performances on stage, a 1986 movie role (in *Private Resort*), a short-lived TV series (NBC's *Tattingers*), some guest shots on series, and more than a decade of struggle as a working actor.

When a visitor, who also was an acquaintance (they'd had one previous conversation, mostly about science fiction), showed up in Roslyn shortly after the actor had gone toe-to-toe with the major studio producing *Northern Exposure* in a very public, very high-stakes contract renegotiation, Morrow was wary and guarded, and not at all inclined to talk publicly. Understandably so, given the negative tone of much of the press coverage around the time of the renegotiations, which often characterized him as ungrateful to the people who'd given him his big break.

"It's not you, man. I like you," he said on more than one occasion on location. "It's the principle of the thing."

For an insider, used to seeing how actors (unknown and otherwise) are routinely manipulated, it was a principle easy to sympathize with. And for his fellow actors, it was a principled stand from which they, too, benefited. As more than one member of the production noted, "when Rob got them to raise his salary, they had to raise *all* the actors' salaries."

Eventually, though, Morrow decided it was okay to talk, and on the morning of the Emmys, the phone rang in a writer's Hollywood apartment. Rob Morrow was on the line.

Do you remember the first time you wanted to be an actor?

I think the first time I was conscious of it was when I was fifteen and saw the movie *Grease*.

You started acting immediately after high school. Does that mean you didn't go to college?

I went to college for about one minute. State College of Northern New Hampshire.

Is it fair to say that when you were a kid, your goal was for a Tony and not an Emmy?

Because of the time in which I did grow up....I always had an eye towards movies, movie work, working with the camera.

[My goal] in New York was to be the best actor I could.

Has the reality of success, fame, and fortune matched the dreams, or is it a nightmare?

No, it's a nice kind of balance of the two. There are nightmarish aspects to it, but far less than the good things. It feels very good to be succeeding in the field that I chose. It's complicated and there's a whole world that you have to learn about, but it's good. I like it.

What are the nightmarish aspects?

It's the politics, it's the business, but that's also just part of growing up, period. I think succeeding, or becoming an adult anywhere, you start to learn about, maybe, some of the greys of life, and the compromises that hopefully are a means to an end.

When you got your fee raised, all the boats rose, right?

I can't talk about it, but I think everyone benefited from what I did. That's what I can say.

Are you on the show for the run of a typical show, five or seven years?

I would think...Dr. Joel's going to be there for a while. We're about to shoot an episode where he gets a year added on to his contract.

It almost seemed to me like the contract dispute that you were having was a publicity ploy to highlight Dr. Joel's contract problems.

If they were smart, they should've taken advantage of that.

Do you have a favorite episode or moment?

Yeah. "Aurora Borealis" [the first-season-ending episode that introduced Chris' brother, Bernard, as well as Adam, Cicely's own Bigfoot].

What did you like about the episode so much?

I love the story line between Bernard and Chris. I think that is the most interesting story ever on television. I think it's funny, and politically correct and interesting, and I just like it.

And the aurora borealis, the way it was shot, there were some really great, expansive [shots].

For some reason, TV people have this idea that you have to keep in the medium or the close shot, and your masters have to be medium master shots....This was a big, panoramic shot of the sky, and they [blue] screened in the aurora borealis. And there was a kind of spirituality and something metaphysical...but it wasn't maudlin.

To me it didn't feel sentimental, even though it was.

Do you want to direct? What are you doing in your spare time?

I *am* directing. I am pursuing things, and will be directing for the show.

I made a short film about a seven-year-old boy in the 1970s, in this kind of Spielbergian village, actually...called *The Silent Alarm*. It's twenty-eight minutes.

I'm going to enter it into the different festivals; it's already gotten into the Seattle Film Festival, and whatever venues there are: cable markets, European markets.

And who's the seven-year-old?

A wonderful, wonderful actor named Jessie Lee Soffer. He turns in a performance almost as good as the kid in Jodie Foster's movie. He's one of those incredibly intelligent, very attractive, very instinctual child actors. He's since gone on to, I guess, do a pilot for someone, and then he's in John Goodman's new movie [*Matinee*], which Joe Dante directed.

Where did you find him?

He just came in through the casting directors in New York....I shot it in New York, and I picked up a day in Seattle because I hadn't finished. Some insert shots over the last year, I picked up.

Can you give me the one-sentence pitch line?

It's about this kid in 1970 in this idyllic town, whose home gets invaded by a man selling alarms door-to-door, and the man ends up moving in and having an affair with this kid's mom. Wreaking

havoc on this kid's psyche, unbeknownst to the mom.

And then it spirals into a very, very veiled child-abuse thing, and eventually the mom picks up on it and has to have the man thrown out.

But what's unusual about it is not so much the story, as opposed to the way I told it. I told it as subjectively as I could and without dialogue.

What do you bring to the part of Dr. Joel? What's Rob and what's written?

I think that wherever I possibly can, maybe sometimes I'm guilty of some transgressions, but wherever I can, I try to play *against* his belligerence. I try to find the essence of the person, as opposed to what's written; it's his kind of defensive posturing. And hopefully that makes him somewhat sympathetic...

Can you give an example?

It's not so much where you could see the broad effect. But sometimes I'll have a line, like, Maggie will come walking into the bar in this beautiful dress and she'll say "Do you notice anything different?"

And I'll say, "Well, those shoes make you look a little bit taller."

And she'll say, "No, no the dress," and I say "Oh, yeah, it's a nice dress."

And I'll try to play something like that...as innocently and as gentle as I can, as opposed to playing into the obvious jibe. Because it just becomes monotonous, and I don't quite understand that aspect of the character a lot.

It seems he's smart enough to know that there's no reason to be that mean. So I'll try to play against it.

And since the text is the text, the balance between actor and text then creates, hopefully, a human being.

How has the character evolved over the couple of years?

I think he's found a fondness for the people of the town. Begrudgingly, obviously. I'd say that's the biggest way he's changed. He's experienced much more of himself, and he may be incrementally wiser.

Do you think the arc of the character is such that there will come an episode where he's freed from the contract and decides to stay?

I would imagine, knowing Josh [Brand] he wouldn't do that. He may leave it ambiguous, but I think that—even though television has certain inherent rules, dramaturgically—I think that Josh fancies trying to play against the expected wherever possible.

The obvious is to think that he will turn and say, "You know what, maybe I'll stay a little while."

That's what I would think he would do, but I think Josh would have him say, "I'm out of here." And bolt, and freeze-frame him running for the bus.

JANINE TURNER
(MAGGIE O'CONNELL)

In person, most of the Beautiful People who are famous from movies or TV simply aren't. At least not as beautiful as they appear on screen. Call it the Magic of Hollywood.

Up close, it's the rare actress who's more striking or prettier than on screen. But exquisitely featured Janine Turner, who plays Maggie O'Connell, Cicely's self-reliant bush pilot, is one of these rare, radiant real-life beauties.

Like Maggie, Janine doesn't trade on her looks, relying instead on a brainy professionalism seemingly beyond her years. Observe, for example, the tireless and apparently genuine cordiality with which she greets the scores of fans watching from across the street, when she finishes filming a scene one morning outside The Brick, on location in Roslyn, Washington:

The little girl on vacation with her family sees a role model; the matronly lady clucks approvingly at the pleasant and proper young actress; the teenage boy looks about to swoon. They all get eye contact, a handshake and a smile; a few words and an autograph if they ask for one; and they all get their picture taken with twinkly, smiley Maggie O'Connell.

Unlike Maggie, Janine *isn't* a pilot, but her father is. In fact, he teaches flying in Texas, where she was raised.

Does your father ever give you any tips on how to play Maggie?

Some. One thing he said is that—and I learned from the statement, I don't know if I necessarily agree with it or not—but being that he teaches flying, he says that women have a tendency not to be as good pilots as men. Cause they tend to react emotionally, and you have to really keep calm in a crisis....He has some fabulous stories though.

Like what?

He was up flying—I think it was a B58, but I don't know: where one's in one bubble and there's another guy behind you in another bubble—and they were up there, and something happened.

I don't remember what, something was going wrong with the plane, and he was feeling a little nervous. He heard this voice—his father had died, I guess, two or three years earlier—and he heard this voice that said "hold on, Tex."

He didn't know where it came from. They got through and they landed, and he turned to his copilot behind him and said, "Did you say something to me?"

He says no, and he asks people down on the ground, you know, did they say anything? No.

So it just gave me chills, because he thinks that perhaps his father was up there saying "Hold on, Tex."

How did you get on the show? Did you ever think it would be such a big success?

Sure is nice. Well, you never know with TV, no, not really, you never know.

I'm one of the firm believers that because we were [first on during] summer, we were able to take more risks, and be more intelligent, and take chances.

If we had been primetime, I think they may have said, "No, no, no, it's got to be more mainstream." The fact it caught on is great—it shows that people were hungry for that kind of television show. So I just got into it by hanging in there basically.

I was living in New York, doing the struggling New York actor deal, I'd been there for four years studying with my coach....So that's what I was doing. Studying. That was the best thing I ever did.

```
                                  March 6, 1990, N.Y.C.

Yellow petals fall to the floor
Stepped on running through the door
To awaiting yellow buds in " sun room "
Ahhhhh, delicious Texas beauties..
In full bloom -
Thank God they come in dozens....
Haven't you met Penny..
Oh.... ( so many )
Yellow petals call from floor
Simply easier to ignore
A dime a dozen..
There are more.
                                  Janine Turner
```

I moved [to New York] when I was twenty-three. And I've been at it since I was fifteen...and I was twenty-seven when I got the part.

I was morbidly depressed [at the time]. I had eight dollars left, just about ready to hang it all up, thinking I had made the wrong decision, cause I turned down a lot of things that I didn't think were quality.

I was holding out for quality. And they gave me [a script], well, all I knew was that she was a pilot. I remember loving the title.

And I went in to the audition and proceeded to leave and cry, tears streaming down my face...

Because you thought you'd blown it?

Yeah, I thought I'd blown it, walking down Park Avenue with my sister-in-law, who I made go into the room with me.

I've never done that before, I'd never been that down. They flew me out to L.A. the next day. I went straight to the network because I had already met all the Universal [Television] people. And I got the part.

I was actually, I was having dry heaves over my toilet back in New York.

Have you changed since the show started?

Life is much more serene....People say, aren't your parents proud? I say, mainly they're *relieved* that I have a job with somebody.

I think it's given me a fabulous opportunity to actually have a creative outlet with my acting. I wrote a lot of poetry during my four years in New York, and I haven't written a poem in a year and a half. Maybe that's because I have a creative outlet. So maybe I'm a happier person. And I've been able to buy a horse.

What kind of horse is it?

She's a Palomino [named "Maggie"].

Are you a horse woman or do you just ride for pleasure?

I ride for pleasure, but someday I'd love to have a big ranch with lots of horses on it, and long-horned cows. And that's nice now, too, I mean the show's given me the opportunity to dream about the kind of thing that before I couldn't even dream about. And it's opened doors for me as far as other opportunities are concerned [e.g. costarring with Sylvester Stallone in *Cliffhanger*].

What's it like to be a single woman in Seattle who's in TV? Are you able to have a personal life?

Well, last year, the hours were so long, I didn't feel like I had a social life at all. Other than sleeping, working and seeing my horse...there didn't seem to be much time for anything else.

But this year, I decided I was going to have a social life, and do things, and just forfeit sleep if I had to. So now I'm trying to get out...do the ferry-boat rides, and enjoy the water.

Can you move around Seattle without being accosted?

No.

What do the fans say to you? Do you get a lot of mail?

Yeah.

Are there themes, like marriage proposals?

I have a few marriage proposals. An astronaut sent me a letter once....He just said that he enjoyed the show, and that if I'm ever in town...I admire that kind of guts, I do. But it's just hard, I can't really go to the supermarket.

I don't mind if people come up, because usually it's, "I enjoy the show very much, and I love your character Maggie," and ninety-eight percent of the time it's really great.

But then some guy was kind of hanging out and waiting for me, and it was dark, and that gets a little scary. And it's different if you're with somebody that's not used to it.

Do people impose on you, like when you're eating?

Yeah, yeah, it's amazing. But I've always kept it in perspective—it goes along with the business and it's better than being broke and unemployed.

Do you remember when it first hit you that this was a big, big hit?

It still is a little hard to believe, and keep it in perspective. Sometimes I wake up and say—I tend to down play it a lot, and keep my life simple and earthy—and yet sometimes I step back and say, "You might as well appreciate it, and kind of own it, and see it, because it doesn't always last forever."

But we're up here in Seattle, so it's a little bit remote. We're not down with all the hoop-da-la in L.A. or New York, which I think has it's good points. It keeps us a little fresh.

How has the part evolved, and what have you brought to it?

Oh, God. Maggie and Janine become one after a while. But I would say in the beginning Maggie was...if I can see transitions that Maggie's made, then perhaps I can make observations as to what I thought that transition was.

I think in the second season you got to see a little more of a sense of humor; she lightened up a little bit. And that was refreshing, that was a lot of fun. Cause they were very stern on me the first eight [episodes] to be, you know, I think they wanted to make sure that Maggie was tough enough.

Maggie has more of an edge, more of a wall than I think I tend to have. And I have that Southern quality that she doesn't have at all. So maybe I've just brought a little bit of mellowing to Maggie, perhaps, over the years. And I struggle to bring emotion to her. My challenge with Maggie, and with the producers, [is] to let there be an occasional tear.

Is there going to be another boyfriend who gets killed off?

I hope not. Wouldn't it be nice if there was one who got better?

JOHN CORBETT

(CHRIS-IN-THE-MORNING)

Now that John Corbett is well on his way to becoming ubiquitous—his iconic image enticing us to buy jeans and his laconic Chris-in-the-Morning voice urging us to buy cars—and his power to turn otherwise sober women into dewy-eyed babblers, obsessing over his hunkiness, has been amply celebrated on the covers of weekly and monthly magazines, it may be hard to recall that he was barely in *Northern Exposure*'s pilot episode—only a couple of quick cutaways, that is, reaction shots of Chris Stevens in the crowd listening as Maurice Minnifield welcomes them to the "ninth annual Arrowhead County Summer Wonderland Festival."

Chris's off-camera voice was in another, earlier scene, and although the scene's still in the pilot [the one where Joel, out of breath from running seven miles into town, asks Ruth-Anne for a bagel and cream cheese and she replies, deadpan, "What's a bagel?"], Chris's voice was left on the cutting room floor.

These are the deleted lines, Chris Stevens's real first appearance in *Northern Exposure*.

CHRIS (off-camera)
(Southern accent)
This is Chris Stevens coming to you on K-BEAR radio from Cicely, Alaska, in the heart and soul of Arrowhead County and you were listening to a cut off of David Byrne's "Rei Momo" album. This morning we're starting our annual countdown toward the Summer Wonderland Festival. On a sorry note, Ray Onetka's prize dogfish, Bonnie, passed away last night. As you all know, Bonnie was two-time defending champion of the Ugly Fish Contest. On a happier note, we'd like to congratulate Greg and Marsha

Weed on their ninth wedding anniversary, Annie O'Shea on her sixth birthday, and we here at the Minnifield Communications Network would also like to extend a hearty welcome to New York City's Joel Fleischman—Arrowhead County's very own physician. This one's for you, Doctor.

And then he plays Frank Sinatra, belting out "New York, New York."

Like perhaps no other character on the show, Chris-in-the-Morning has *caught on*. Big time.

As they did with Marilyn Whirlwind, the show's writers were smart enough, practically from the get-go, to write *to* Chris and draw *on* John. It's no accident that Chris, like John, grew up in Wheeling, West Virginia; that they both had the same childhood friends and relatives (Uncle Roy, Chuck Vincent, and Earl P. Duffy, among others); and that what Chris wears around Cicely are basically the same clothes that John bops around in back in town. They both have a Harley, too.

That John put in six years on the line at a steel factory, or worked as a hairdresser in a Hollywood salon are biographical details that also could fit Chris's checkered past. John caught the acting fever in a class at Cerritos Community College, near L.A., after a back injury ended a promising career as a welder and pipe fitter.

Before *Northern Exposure* there were some fifty commercials and a guest shot on *The Wonder Years*.

How did you get the part?

Well, I had been auditioning for about two years trying to get a pilot. I had done *The Wonder Years* in '88, their fourth episode ever, and they weren't even on the air yet. When it came out, it

was a nice guest-starring role. I had gotten a lot of meetings [from it], and ABC offered me a talent-developing deal, which we—me and my team—didn't take.

So I was trying to get a series, and it was about two years. I went in, I would get close to things, and nothing would pan out. This was '90, and I hadn't worked.

I had just gotten really close. Janine, also, had gotten really close, on this pilot Tom Selleck was producing, called *Heat*.

I thought, *This is it, I'm going to be a big star, I'm going to get this TV show, and it shoots in Hawaii,* and you know, that was going to do it.

It fell through, and one other big thing fell through for me.

I was depressed. It was the end of pilot season in '90, and I knew it was going to be a long wait until the next one. Then the gig came up.

My agent called and said, "There's a new show called *Northern Exposure*, about a doctor that comes to Alaska."

So I got the script, and I read it, and I didn't think I could play a doctor, a Jewish doctor in Alaska. So I called him back and said, "That's a great script, man, it's one of the best ones I've ever read, but I'm not right for this."

He said, "What do you mean?"

I said, "You know I can't play this, there's a million guys out there that can play this kind of role, and it's not me."

And he said, "The deejay, right?"

And I said, "No, the doctor." Because, you know, I had gone through the cast and it's not the astronaut, and it's not Holling, it's surely not Ed the Indian. And it was like, that was the only other male character. And he said, "No, there's a deejay. He's kind of this philosophical guy."

Well, in the first script, there was one little monologue that I had just skimmed over. I just read it and went on, because I had been doing it for leads and things, right? And this was literally one page. I just fucking went over it.

I thought they were trying to get me up for Joel. And so I went back and read it on page, whatever it was, and I said, "Yeah, it's kinda interesting, it's small—it's one page!—but I haven't worked. I'm ready to work."

So I went in, and they liked me.

Josh and John [the show's creators]....We just kind of sat around, and they were interesting looking. They were young, and we kind of hit it off. We didn't talk much, we didn't chit-chat too much. They were sort of quiet and checking me out. And I sat in a chair just like this and just kind of read. They had some Walt Whitman they wanted me to read.

They brought me back three times, and the next thing you know, like a week and a half later, I was at the network. It was scary.

When you get turned away as an actor, it's you they are rejecting. How do you handle that, and what did you do to support yourself?

To support myself I did TV commercials. So I didn't have to have another job. How to deal with the rejection? Good buddies, good friends, who I'd go out with at night, and we'd have a good laugh. I'd just laugh, just *laugh*. We'd make jokes all night long, and I'd feel good and be ready to go to work the next day trying to get a job.

Go to work—not being paid to go to work, but, you know, trying to get a job, drum up an audition, find out if a movie is being made.

You're basically doing the same thing before people like you as after people like you. Is it hard to keep doing it now that people like you?

No. It's just the same. It's *exactly* the same. My whole process about how I work as an actor, how I go about getting a job, what I do in between. There's only one little twist in there now. People recognize me on the street. That's the only twist, everything else is exactly the same.

When you're struggling and you imagine yourself as successful, is the reality what you imagined it to be?

Right now it's sort of indifferent, it's just sort of the ways things are. At first it was better, then it got worse, and now it's kind of just even-keeled out, because it's been two years.

What's the best part of being famous or successful?

The best part about being successful...is the financial part. I don't have to do some slasher movie just because the bucks are low, and have to justify it as, Hey, it's an okay part. So I don't have to do that—and never had to, fortunately. I got lucky. And people consider me now [for parts], because I'm on this show that's a quality show...

I get to go in now and meet top-notch directors, and not deal with the casting director or the casting director's assistant like I used to, or try to sneak by the studio and submit myself while somebody's at lunch, which I've done before.

That's interesting...What's the weirdest thing you did?

I hijacked a movie. I was up for a part in a movie called *The Flight of the Intruder*, a Paramount movie.

I was up for a nice part in that, and the casting

people...kept bringing me back....And my friend Jared...was an actor, had done some stuff for movies and was perfect for this. But they couldn't see him.

I had been getting familiar with the guard-gate guys every day. So I got my friend Jared—this is great—I got Jared to get down in front of the car, he had a '57 Chevy, so he's down in the front seat. And I come driving in and kind of wave to the guys and go, "Hey, back again," and they go, "Okay, okay, you know where it is."

So I sneak Jared over, and nobody's in the casting office right now, so we plant some of his pictures around, right? And we split and get out of there. Then I get on the phone and tell [the casting director] "You've got to see this guy," and she's like, "Yeah, his pictures are popping up all over the place, who is he?"

To make a long story short, he gets cast in a major role in this picture, and I get booted out. I don't get a thing.

So they're over in Hawaii shooting—Willem Dafoe's in it, Danny Glover—and I get a call, and they go, "Hey, John, it's a small part, but we want you to be in the movie. Can you be one of the pilots?"

I said, "Absolutely." So I got to work on this movie for like six weeks, and was on the *USS Independence*, the aircraft carrier, going up and down the coast; had some really nice scenes.

I'm basically a featured extra now, but I'm in there. I'm like thirteenth down in the credits.

Do you remember when you first wanted to be an actor?

Yes, and no. Ever since I was a kid I always enjoyed watching movies, more than most kids.

I remember watching *It's a Wonderful Life*, ever since I was a little kid, and *The Wizard of Oz*, and, like, really being blown away by the sort of technical aspect of it. I remember being just a little kid and watching *The Wizard of Oz* and knowing that somehow it wasn't real, that it was on a big soundstage somewhere, and trying to find flaws.

I eventually read, just a couple of years ago, that *The Wizard of Oz* is one of the most flawless movies ever made. I think they've gone through it with a fine-tooth comb and found like two flaws. Like maybe a Munchkin's wearing a watch.

But it [acting] didn't happen until my mid-twenties...

You can't be much older than that now.... How old are you?

I never tell my age. But I was in my mid-twenties when I discovered what I wanted.

Do you find most of the stuff written about you is bull, or are you given a fair shake in the press?

I've had two things in the tabloids that weren't true at all. One was linking me with someone romantically, and the other was that I had a wife and two kids who were handicapped....I've never been married. But all the other stuff...is all legit.

Do you have a favorite episode?

I've got a couple. One of my favorites is "Spring Break," where we all ran naked at the end. There was a scene I did with Darren Burrows [Ed] on the radio station, and [co-executive producer] Rob Thompson directed. That was the first time Rob had come up and directed a show. And there was a scene at the end in the radio station where [Ed] catches me with, ah, the goods. That's one of my favorite scenes. And also another one that Rob Thompson directed ["Burning Down the House"], where we flung a piano. And that whole show was a real special one.

Is there anything that you want Chris to do that he hasn't done yet?

I'd like to explore some martial arts maybe.

Do you do martial arts?

No, no, I don't do them at all. But I'd like for Chris to be a martial artist in a way, and maybe get in a fight and whip someone's ass. You know, real passively though.

Something like that might be kind of fun. A little action. But other than that I'm still happy with the way they are going.

Is there anything you've felt uncomfortable doing, anything you've been uncomfortable saying?

No . . . I love this kind of stuff. Anything out of the ordinary.

As much as I love being in the booth, if I can get out and do a scene with someone, *that's* where the bread and butter is for me, because I like reacting with people, and doing a scene.

It gets lonely in that booth sometimes, just kind of doing my monologues.

What about that tattoo story?

That was one of the things I did when I first got the character, when I went in to meet those guys [Josh Brand and John Falsey, the show's cocreators].

They said he was this ex-con, and I envisioned this hard kind of a guy. And you know I'm soft-spoken and laid back, and I'm not very intimidating. I'm tall but I'm not intimidating.

So I put these tattoos all over my arm. I got a book and I really went to town and spent like an hour-and-a-half, two hours, making these detailed [drawings], with this green pen that looked just like tattoo ink. And I painted all these tattoos.

Then I got wet paper towels and [made] them look really aged. So I went in with my flannel shirt rolled, smoking a smoke, kind of had my hair hanging down like this, and didn't say too much. I was just trying to find the character, trying to be something that I wasn't.

So I end up telling them that these weren't real, and they didn't believe me, so I had to wet one and show them the ink.

And I'm glad . . . when we first got up here [to Seattle], I said to Josh, "Do you want me to do the tattoo thing?"

He was kind of considering it. I'm glad he didn't now, because it would be a pain in the ass.

What does John bring to Chris?

I bring everything. My whole life.

You tend to read exactly what's in the script, I've noticed, but you give the reading something that I can't articulate. What is it that you're doing there?

I don't know really. I memorize the thing, sort of verbatim. And then I just throw it away and sit down in the booth and, I don't try to give a memorized monologue, I just kind of talk. And maybe see some images in my mind. That's about it, really.

How do you find the character? Do you do method, or do you need to find how the character is dressed, how do you do it?

They give me a lot of leeway. Most of the stuff I get to wear, all this jewelry and the clothes, most of them are mine. I do my own hair. My hair just looks like this usually.

They've just given me so much leeway. I just show up in the morning and go sit in the booth or do a scene, and throw my clothes on. So I kind of feel like myself when I go out there. People still refer to me as Chris all the time, even directors

I'm working with. They call me Chris and they don't catch themselves. I don't know, really, because it's not me. I'm just doing the scene, memorizing the words, but I try to do them in a way that it's totally like I'm having a conversation...

What do you know about the character that we don't know?

I've created my own little history in my mind, so I can play certain things, but I get a lot out of the scripts. I find out new things all the time.

They let my character be from where I'm from, which is Wheeling, West Virginia; and they let me constantly refer to people I knew and grew up with.

Really? Like who?

Like Greg "The Joy King" George, who is my best friend back there. He's got a wife and kids. Roy Bower, another good friend of mine, who I went to grade school with, but in [the show] I call him my Uncle Roy Bower—I mention his passing away.

My buddy Chuck, Chuck Vincent. Who else? The Dean of Discipline.

I went to Catholic school for twelve years—and we had a guy there named Earl P. Duffy, and his official title was the Dean of Discipline. So this last [episode] we just did, I got to talk about Earl P. Duffy.

And I talk about Wheeling constantly.... They get a big kick out of that.

Do you still have family there?

Yeah. My dad lives in Southern California, my mother in West Virginia.

Did your parents support you going into acting?

I worked in a steel factory after high school, I came to California and met my real dad. He worked for the boilermakers union, so I worked in a steel factory for about six years, and I hurt my back—which is bothering me today, I'm trying to crack it—then I went to a junior college, and that's where I discovered acting.

So I was on my own, I had been living on my own for years, and I was just sort of doing it on my own, not really telling anybody what I was doing by that point.

Do you remember the first time you felt like a success?

After *The Wonder Years*. The next two or three weeks after *The Wonder Years* premiered, I did.

I signed a lot of autographs. I'd walk down the street and people'd go, "Oh, man, you're Lewis," and I'd say, "Yeah."

That was kind of neat, that was my first taste. And then, like I said, it went away for two years, really quick. But, believe it or not, people still come up to me and they go, "I know you from the show, but you were great in *Wonder Years*"...I did one episode.

Now are you living in Seattle? Do you have a house?

No, I just rent an apartment, right down the road....I've got a house in Pasadena.

What would you like to do after Northern Exposure?

I don't know. I enjoy acting....I do music, I actually enjoy that more than acting...I've recorded some stuff, I'm in touch with some labels, so we'll see about signing....It's country rock, kind of like John Cougar....Dwight Yoakam-ish.

I would like to go in that direction. I'm not so sure about the acting. I like it, it's fine, but it's sort of not as fulfilling as probably at one time I thought it would be.

Is that because it's TV, or would movies be the same?

My process is the same. With any role. Even when I did those plays in college theater, I did like five or six plays, it's exactly the same.

I don't know if I have to find another way of working or if it's just sort of not for me. But I just can't get so excited about it.

It's always at a certain level for me. I never get really excited about, you know, "Hey, let's rehearse this scene!" Or, "This is going to be a great play!" Or, "Boy, this episode's going to be really good!"

It's fun while we do it, and then the day's long, and it's fourteen hours, and then you go home and forget about it. And then it comes on TV a couple months later, and you watch it, and it takes an hour of your time from ten to eleven, and then that thrill's gone. And you know, the thrills don't keep coming, you know what I mean?

What was the worst moment on the show for you?

There was one. I had to say—and Rob Thompson and I still joke about this. I had to say "Swami Bodhidharma," and I kept saying "Swodi Boderramma." And to this day he keeps saying to me, "Hey, Swodi," and I'll go, "Hey, Swodes…"

You and Janine are very good with the fans. Do you like that aspect of it?

Yeah. They come out there [to Roslyn] because they want to come there. And for us to jump in a van and kind of whiz by, when they've come so far to see us; you know, it takes me all of seven minutes to go over there and sign some autographs and shake their hand and take a picture.

And you know, I get something out of it too, it makes me feel nice. I love the fans. Because they love us…

BARRY CORBIN

(MAURICE MINNIFIELD)

Barry Corbin may be fixed firmly in our minds now as Maurice Minnifield, ex-astronaut and First Citizen of Cicely, Alaska, but for more than a decade before *Northern Exposure*, he was a respected character actor, the quintessential look-it's-what's-his-name, with roles in more than one hundred films and television shows.

You've seen him in everything from *Urban Cowboy* and *Lonesome Dove* to *The Man Who Loved Women* and *The Thorn Birds*. He also teaches at Texas Tech and has written plays for National Public Radio.

Corbin's an avid horseman. On the day he rides up to the show's nondescript soundstage in suburban Seattle on his newest horse, he's the very picture of an Old West cowboy, riding tall on a hand-tooled monogrammed saddle; his Stetson white, his beard stubbly, and his eyes steely behind aviator shades. He's wearing worn leather chaps over faded jeans, a red Western shirt with white trim and black cowboy boots with red trim and jingly silver spurs.

Later, after he's trotted down the road, crew members assure a city-slicker visitor that Barry rides up from a nearby stables dressed that way "all the time."

You've done so much TV, so many movies. How is Northern Exposure *different than what you've done before?*

The work's always the same. The fundamentals of the work. Sometimes the scripts are better. Sometimes you have more time to explore other avenues at work.

In feature films usually you have more time to explore things a little more before you dive in and make a final choice. In television, you're pretty much by the seat of your pants.

You commit to a choice and you go with it, because there's no time to explore. You don't have time in rehearsal, you don't have time to explore the various ramifications of the scene. Sometimes it gets you in trouble, because you realize you made the wrong choice, and you've got to play that choice.

Can you give me an example of that?

Not a specific example in this case, but I can give you a hypothetical example. If you have made a choice to play a scene—your overall performance is an arc—and if you peak too soon in the arc, you'll have a performance that [goes flat].

If, say, you're playing a very dramatic piece, and your brother is killed and then your mother dies, well, it can't be the same thing, it can't be *both* equal weight. Your brother being killed, because it comes first, should be in the arc of your performance, on your way up; you're traumatized by it. But the death of your mother, because it happens later, should be stronger.

In a television show, you might be in a rush: they might film the brother's death first and you hit your peak there, and you can't top it with your mother's death.

How broadly do you play? TV is a tight-shot medium...

If the thoughts behind it are honest thoughts, you can play as broad as you want to play. If you're simply playing attitude—some kind of broad stroke—or if you don't have a through-line [i.e., a theme] in the scene, any broadness is phony.

Maurice could easily be caricature, but he's very affecting, touching.

That's because he's alone. That's because he is a person who is solitary. He's lonely. He's a sensitive man in that he knows what his likes are. He, at first glance, seems a very *in*sensitive guy. But he's a man of contradictions: he could become a buffoon, he could become a stock villain, he could become any number of things. We always have to keep the balance there.

How do you find the character? Are the clothes important to you? Is it important that you think of something in your personal life that reminds you of something about Maurice?

Each character you play is different. The way I work, I read the script, without any predisposition, I read the script as if I'm reading a novel.

People are complex organisms, therefore I figure the character is a complex organism. If it's a caricature, I can usually tell that about ten pages in. Then I skim the rest of it and see if there are any surprises, and put it away.

If they are complex, I don't make a judgment. If a person does bad things, I don't assume it's a bad person, I don't assume that it's a monster. There are no monsters.

If a person is a monster, is completely irredeemable, in his own eyes as well as everybody else's, if he's evil for evil's sake, then I don't want to play the part. I have no interest in playing that, any more than I would have an interest in playing someone that is just good. You've got to have contradictions in order to have a fully rounded human being.

All the characters in *this* show have contradictions.

What do you think it is about the show that's caught the public's fancy?

It's a combination of a whole lot of things that causes the show to catch the imagination of the public. I thought it had the potential. But I've done four or five series before, and they've never gone past thirteen [episodes]. I've never done a pilot that I haven't thought was good.

Did you see this role as a good opportunity right away?

Well, to commit yourself to seven years, you have to think about it, you have to weigh the situation.

In this particular case, we were contracted to do eight episodes in the summer. There was an outside possibility for the fall, which they didn't [do]; then there was an outside possibility that they might pick up some more [episodes] for mid-season replacement, which they really didn't do. They picked up eight more at the end of the season. So if it was going to be killed, that would have killed it...

I thought, Yeah, it would be a hit. Because it's a different kind of a show, and it's got something for everybody and never talks down to anybody.

There's a genuine caring for each other in the characters. They all care for each other—they might not understand each other, but they all care for each other.

Do you have a favorite moment?

No, I couldn't pick one...I like the one where Holling and I went and got our buddy, Bill, I liked that one because I enjoy shooting outside. [The episode, which aired originally on March 2, 1992, was titled "Three Amigos."]

When you and Holling are together, it has the feel of a classic Western.

Um-hum. I think we could make a pretty good Western....But I think there were moments in "Seoul Mates" that were good. There was a moment in the first season when I talked on the

radio about why we need our heroes, which I liked. That moment, I liked a lot.

What do you bring to Maurice? I get the sense that, as the series went on, the writers started writing "to you."

Oh, I think they probably did. I'm not aware of it, but I think that's natural. I think they probably did that for all of us.

Maybe for Cynthia [Geary, who plays Shelly Tambo] less, because her character is so different from what she is. And all of our characters are different from what we are. I mean John Cullum is not like Holling. And I'm not like Maurice...

Well, you sound like Maurice...

Oh, we sound alike, we look alike, but that's about it....But the edges start to blur.

What would you like to see happen to Maurice? Will he ever get the girl?

Oh, I think that would be a bad mistake. To cure him of his loneliness I think would be a bad mistake. I think they are going to have [Officer] Barbara [Semanski] come back...which is good, I'm glad to hear that.

Do you have astronaut groupies the way Maurice does?

I've got the women writing to me about their dreams, and their erotic thoughts.

Oh, really? Do you answer them?

Oh, I try to answer them ambiguously. I usually answer all my letters eventually.

What do the fans say to you?

They mostly don't think I'm Maurice.

Tell me about teaching at Texas Tech.

I go in and do a seminar about every two years. Professional theater, acting in film, acting in television.

And you're a writer. Do you do any prose writing?

Oh yeah. I've gotten a couple of plays published. I haven't written any books. I've started some short stories that I haven't ever really polished. Plays and radio plays mostly.

Is your character in any way based on the Jack Nicholson character in Terms of Endearment?

I don't think so. Now, that character is kind of a drunk, kind of irresponsible. I mean Maurice is way down on responsibility. He's *absolutely* the most responsible human being you can find. For somebody who has nobody to be dependent on him, his whole thought is of immortality.

The town is his family.

Well, he considers himself the patriarch, everybody else considers him a pain in the ass.

JOHN CULLUM

(HOLLING VINCOEUR)

The man who portrays the man who owns The Brick is a distinguished, Tony-winning stage actor who's trod the boards with the likes of Burton and others, the best in the business.

He was nominated for Broadway's most-coveted honor for his first starring role in *On a Clear Day You Can See Forever* and won his first Tony as Best Actor in a Musical in 1976 for *Shenandoah*.

Oddly enough, his rugged leading-man good looks are more apparent in person than on TV. Cullum and Holling, though, seem to share a certain courtliness and a thoughtfulness of demeanor.

TV is a producer's medium, film is a director's medium. What about the stage?

The stage is a star's medium, or a director's medium, or an ensemble's medium. It really depends on what the script is or who's connected to it. And it depends on where it's being done.

For instance, when I did *On the Twentieth Century*, I tried to hide from [director] Hal Prince—this is the truth...because I didn't like the script, and I knew the play, the Ben Hecht play. I didn't think it worked, cause it was all staged on a train...

Prince finally said, "John I want you to see something." He took me over and he showed me the set, he showed me the way it worked. And I said, "Okay, I'll do the show...because now I know who the star is, the star is Fred Wagner, the set designer. The star is the set."

***You anticipate my last question. Who or what is the star of* Northern Exposure?**

Um. See, I've been with it now for two years, and my opinion has begun to change over it...[at first] I thought it was the characters, and I thought it was the locale, and I thought it was the juxtaposition of the New York sophisticate against these raw, kind of savages, so to speak, who instinctively knew the right things to do, or had big hearts.

And so they came off better, and his foibles and faults were reflected more blatantly because of them. That's what I thought this show was all about. And the general good nature of these people that naturally happens in a frontier kind of situation. All of these things I thought made this show work, and I think all of those things contribute to it.

I thought that Josh and John, in a strange way, borrowed ideas a lot, took ideas from other things. And I didn't necessarily approve of that, but I looked at it as an interesting kind of thing.

Now I'm beginning to believe that that *is* part of the system. This is going to get pretty erudite, I don't want to sound too esoteric here, but you know, the way that...if you read Shakespeare, or you read any good writer, really, you get a lot of literary references? Or if you look at a painter, you get reflections of other painters and writers and things? And they use that almost as a vocabulary. And it never occurred to me that these guys write for television.

And we have a lot of what, when I first look at it, is sort of cliché ideas, things that you wouldn't dwell on in a stage production.

Give me an example of what you mean.

Well, um, just simply the situations. Take for instance my situation: the old guy and the young girl—a built-in, immediate, fast response that you get right away. And it's fresh in one way, but it's an old-fashioned, clichéd kind of thing. Once it's done, then you think you should move on. We use it. Now, it's there all the time.

Who or what is the star as we speak?

The concept. That's the conclusion that I've come to over a long period of time.

It's like how I always used to talk about Hal Prince. Hal Prince is not a very good director in my opinion. But Hal Prince had his finger on the pulse of the situation—he knew what New Yorkers, and he knew what theater was about during the time—and as long as it was all a toy to him, as long as he was having fun doing it, he knew how to produce, and direct and put together shows that were hits on Broadway, because that's what the public wanted.

When you say that Josh and John put in references and borrow, you're not talking about Chris-in-the-Morning and reading excerpts from Jack London?

Yes. That's part of it. And also, when we started using things out of *Twin Peaks*. And dream sequences in which we play characters out of movies, where we borrow ideas from TV. You see, when I was first starting the show, I found that offensive almost, and I thought of it as almost being plagiarism. But then I started thinking about it: if it works, then what is it? If it's not what I think it is, then what is it? So I've come to the conclusion that it's a concept.

It's the same thing Shakespeare did.

Exactly. He uses the Greeks. He uses things that are prevalent at the time, like psychology, and melancholy was a big thing right at the time he was writing...I'm beginning to say, Hey, wait a minute, this thing *works*, why does it work?

And I think it's because it has a vocabulary, it draws on past things that people understand. We no longer have people that know Milton and

Paradise Lost and even the Bible, which is the biggest reference that we have always had in our country. Shakespeare and the Bible and Emerson...You ask what kids [know]...they don't even know when the Civil War was. They think the Civil War was before the Revolutionary War.

You've done film, you've done theater, and now you're doing TV. What do you like best? Tell me some of the differences.

Just learning how to do the technique of television has been a kind of revelation; I don't think I'm very good in television.

What I was referring to is the changes, how do you emote differently when you're talking to a camera and to an audience?

It's just like us sitting here, the way we're talking. As an actor, if I were performing for you...I would adjust my performance, because we are by ourselves, and I am probably acting to a certain extent right now.

I've performed for houses of twenty-five, and I've performed for houses of twenty-five-thousand, and the technique of course changes, but not really...

Television, though, and film, is a lot different than I thought it was. I used to think all you have to do is cut back, and use that same technique. It's not true. You've got more things working for you as an actor in film, than you do on stage.

What you *can't* do on stage is you can't make people see nothing but the eyebrow. On stage, they see the stage, and you have to get their attention and make them focus on what you want them to focus on. In film...it's not necessarily focus, but it's elimination. You get rid of everything that you don't want, and they see what you tell them to see. And the camera does the work for the actor.

That's why Clint Eastwood and Gene Hack-

man...have wonderful film technique, because they can convey emotion and not do very much.

Let's talk about history. How did you get the part...what made you take it?

I think I was in New York. I did the tape, and then met briefly with John and Josh [*Northern Exposure*'s cocreators]. Then they brought me out here to California...

I was going to give California two years, which I've never done. California and I never got along too well....[Earlier, my agents] wanted to know why I wouldn't move out there, and I [had] said, "My wife's a dancer, she has a dance company back there. I'm a Broadway star."...They said, "Who would you rather be, Laurence Olivier or Cary Grant?" And I thought, You stupid son-of-a-bitch, who the fuck do you think I am? Do you think I'm stupid?

And then they said, "You know what you need to do? Your wife doesn't want to come out here? Divorce her." That's the kind of attitude these guys had—these are my own agents—and it's so repulsive to me, and so detached from any kind of significant feeling that I thought was right.

I just got off to a bad start. The wrong people to associate with were the agents.

Tell me the difference between you and Holling? What are the similarities?

Well, our fantasies are the same [*big laugh*]. I think the difference between Holling and me is that he had another life that excluded that particular kind of thing that happened to him at the age of sixty-three, which was this terrifically attractive woman. I don't think he's ever really been that attractive to women. He's an outdoors-man. I think there's a lot more to Holling, I read lots more things into it. He may have had a relationship with another woman...

He did. There's an episode where an old flame shows up and Shelly gets jealous...

Yeah. But she wasn't even really an old flame. I think that there was an old flame, but it's never happened.

They tell me there is an episode coming up where my daughter comes back, and I've been trying to get something like that going, some other part of Holling. But I think the difference between Holling and me—he was totally devoted to another life.

Now, what it was, I think, it may have been, he could have been a killer. I mean, he killed animals. He may have been a man who at some place killed a man, or two. Or maybe he was a hired assassin at one time, in the sense of being a lawman. There's some portion of his life that is cut off, and quiet, and causes a great, deep disturbance.

Holling strikes me as having walked into Cicely from a Western; he's like Unforgiven, the Clint Eastwood Western.

Very much that. Except that in *Unforgiven* it's all out in the open. I don't think we'll ever get it all out in the open with Holling.

You know, our subtext, it's not so horrendous if you get it out in the open, I'm assuming; I guess that's what psychiatrists say. But we all have subtexts.

My subtext has to do with the Southern Baptist upbringing, in a sense with tyranny and the whole thing with the blacks, and prejudice, and everything. My attitude about women, my sexuality and all of that stuff...

I'm saying that kind of underlying guilt and anger and frustration that comes out of southerners, and Southern Baptists, and small family,

small interlocking, this is the subtext for a lot of people.

I'd like to see something that gets close to the dangerous, dangerous element of him, and somehow connect his ability to keep that in check with the relationship to Shelly.

When Dan Quayle took off on Murphy Brown, I thought the next target was going to be the Holling-Shelly relationship.... Are people ever upset about it?

I don't get letters [about it] very often. Usually they are from young people. They love Holling, I don't know why. A father-figure I guess.

That fact that he's in love with a young person, I don't think they think of it in terms of the sexuality necessarily. I told this to somebody the other day, when I'm walking around up there in Roslyn and an older couple comes up to me. The guy gets a kind of shitty grin on his face. And he kind of comes over and says, "I really love your character."

You know, he whispers it to me, and you know that there's a certain amount of guilt. And there are women who don't like the fact that he likes younger women. And there have been one or two occasions when I've been reluctant to say certain lines. And one of them I wouldn't say at all.

What was that?

I did not want to say a line that implied that I liked her simply because she was young and, by implication, I didn't like older women. I just gave it a little different spin.

That wasn't the "I don't like you for your mind, I like you for your body" line?

Not that one. I had problems with that one too. I was going to change that. What happened was, I was so nervous about that scene, I didn't even mention it to anybody. A lot of the things that I had objected to had worked, and I kept worrying about that line, and I learned it the way it was written. And at the last minute I [was] just going to say "I can't do this line," or I was just going to change it.

And then when I was playing the scene, and it was very long, it was hard for me to play, and then suddenly...it came out, not that I didn't *like* her brain, but that I *loved* her body. And that I loved her for being what she was. And I was desperate to assure her that I loved her because of her body. Because she was afraid that I didn't love her because of her body, and so I was reassuring her.

The scene worked because I wanted to make her feel better, and feel my love. And I thought, "Shit, this goddamned thing worked," and so I didn't change it.

That dark side of the character made me think of his relationship with Shelly. Maybe he's afraid that he loves her so much, but that in a certain frame of mind he could hurt her.

I don't think so. Maybe it's because that's not my nature. I might hurt a woman if it was just sex. I don't know my nature in that, but I do know I have certain areas, like all men do I think...but I don't think that I would hurt Shelly. She might drive me to hurt myself.

That southern dark streak could lead to suicide?

Yeah. He has that. If that gets in the [book], I'm going to be dead within the year because it's such a good idea....I'd have to die in the saddle.

How do you find the character? Does it come from the inside? Is it the clothes that the character wears?

I never have been much of that kind of actor, that's like a Laurence Olivier approach to acting. You know something, having said that, I think I *am* affected by those things.

And as far as bringing the character home, I think I bring the character to work, that Holling is affected by me, my moods, and it's easier for me to open up and view Holling with my fears and my anxieties and my passion, than it is to try and figure what Holling is.

How has Holling changed over the course of the show?

I guess he's changed mainly in that I'm allowing myself to go into these areas of myself...

I like to play comedy. I think that Holling has a sense of humor, and I like his sense of humor, but I don't think he's a buffoon, and there's a tremendous temptation to play into the buffoonery. And sometimes it works wonderfully well...but I'm backing away from that.

How have you changed?

I don't think I've changed, except that I'm in the learning process, and I've gotten a lot more appreciation. I'm beginning to know a little bit more of what I don't know. That's pleasurable. It doesn't take much to please me, in terms of work....I like the little changes I've brought to him.

You are saying that Holling knows what he's capable of, and because of that he has to draw back and keep within himself...

You're right. The one area they do get into—it recurs over and over, cause that's what I think most writers like—is Holling is terrified of death. He's like, Patton probably was terrified of death from what I can tell; or a lot of people who are over-heroic, [they] are frightened.

Once you get past that certain age, that

terrifying confrontation, that inevitable thing, is getting closer and closer. I've seen it happen to older people—they are usually very energetic, very driven, very overachievers. But they've never done it, what Hamlet did, at the age of thirty-three, which was to confront it...

Do you have a favorite moment?

The favorite moments usually aren't the best moments. And I've found that's true of most actors. The things that touch me, like when I'm playing it, like nostalgia, or loss of something, or like what we're talking about, a deep-seated thing. If I'm aware of it, and I'm choked up about it and moved by it, and I'm playing it. Unfortunately, when I see that on film, I'm not pleased with what happens.

Do you have trouble watching yourself?

I don't watch it very much. Yes, I do have trouble watching myself. I shouldn't, it's not a big deal. But what I'm saying is not a terrible thing. There are wonderful moments that I like very much. I love Jesse the Bear...

The best moments that I've ever done on stage are ones that I can't remember....When you're really doing good work on stage, or performing, you don't remember it. Literally, you don't remember it. I've said that to my son. Unfortunately, in our business, you don't remember the great moments, because you're so involved in it, that it's not you any more. You're suddenly taken over.

If you were writing an episode, what would you have happen to Holling?

I would like a touch of what we were talking about, some of that dark side of him, the violence that he knows he's capable of. Somehow, rather than connecting my relationship to Shelly with a physical, jump-into-bed-and-fuck-all-the-time—if there was something about the relationship that was my salvation from myself. You'll find that in *Unforgiven*...how poignant and how sensitive strong men who are full of violence can be.

At the beginning Holling and Shelly were a unit, a sort of closed unit. And now Holling's concerns are bigger than Shelly...

I'm glad of that, because that's the way humans behave. When I said about that fast thing that you see—he's an old man and she's a young woman and they love to get in the sack—that epitomizes the first impressions that you have of Holling and Shelly. Then you look at it another way and it gets a little more complicated, when you put them under pressure and watch them react, and we kind of forget that they're older and younger.

They are two people who are in love, and they have to face problems, and they face them in different ways, she as a young person, he as an old person, and yet they *can* get together. I like it when it gets more complicated.

Are you more recognized now than ever before?

I've never had anything like this at all. I like it, it's a great deal of fun. You know, I was a star on Broadway for many years, and I could walk down Broadway and very few people would know who I was.

It doesn't make any difference where I am now...you can't go any place without people recognizing you. They're not offensive. One of the things that I like about Holling is that people are very—they are not standoffish, but they are reluctant to intrude on Holling.

CYNTHIA GEARY

(SHELLY TAMBO)

Cynthia Geary's peppy enough alright, and she's got Shelly Tambo's all-American girl-next-door good looks, too, but that's about where the resemblance ends.

Even wearing Shelly's ditzy retro-sixties-waitress gear and seated primly in the small, plainly furnished mobile home she has on location, Geary projects what Emmy-winning cinematographer Frank Prinzi approvingly calls "this sense of still, deep water." Sunny, serene, yet on point and businesslike. Apparently, the all-American girl coping sensibly with the all-American Hollywood fantasy: As a struggling young actress, she was discovered for the part of Shelly while actually waitressing.

Were you really waitressing before you got the part? Tell me what happened?

I was waitressing and studying acting, and I had just finished college.

Where were you waitressing?

At a Mexican restaurant called El Paso Cantina in L.A., and it closed, it didn't do very well. But I happened to wait on a woman...and her husband, who was an executive with Warner Bros. [She was a] casting director. And of course I didn't know who they were.

I waited on them, and at the end of dinner she said, "Are you an actress?" and I said, "Yeah."

And she said, "Well, here's my card, and call me. I think you have a great personality."

So I took her card, and I didn't know what company she was with. I asked some of my friends, and they said that that was a big company that handled big stars, and you should call her.

About three days later, I called her back and she said, "Where have you been? I didn't know how to get in touch with you, I didn't think I was going to find you. Come in and bring all your tapes."

So I hung up the phone, and like, you know, great, "tapes," what do I do?

And the only thing I had a tape of was *Divorce Court*. I had done that....So I got that and went in and met with her and the head of the company. And they said that they were going to review the tape and "We'll call you back."

But I assumed that that was going to be it, my "big break." But they called me back the next day and I went in to see them again. And they said, "Well, we'd like to handle you, we'd like to represent you, but we're never going to show anybody the tape. And we want to put you with an agency."

I had an agent but they wanted to change my agency. So I said fine...and the next thing I knew, that was my first pilot [reading]...for *Northern Exposure*.

And so from the last time you said, "Will that be all?" to the first time you said "Holling" in front of the camera, how long was that?

Actually, it was about three months, from the time I met her till I read for *Northern Exposure*...I met her in January and I got cast for *Northern Exposure* in April.

Do you remember what she had for dinner?

Well, yeah. Because it was...[her husband's] birthday, and so I gave him free flan, so maybe they thought I was doing something special. I mean, we did that for everybody...

I don't know what entrees I gave them, I just remember I gave them a free dessert, and I'm really glad I did.

Were you going out for parts before and not getting them, or what?

I went up for really small things. My agent wasn't horrible, but I didn't have an agent with enough power to get me in to read for pilots and things like that. I was reading for like, *Rambo Women Go to South America*, and thank God I didn't get any of them.

I look too nice or something, but I never got any of those movies. Actually, I did. I had one line in three bad B-movies, they were teenager movies. I don't mean "bad" as in morally bad, just bad, commercially, crummy movies. So that was it. I count myself very lucky to have run into the right people.

Well, luck favors the well-prepared...

Well, I agree. I *definitely* agree. I think that everybody, no matter what you do, has got to have a lucky break. I mean someone's got to give you the chance to show that you can do it. But you've got to be prepared for it.

I studied, and I studied really hard. I was the kind that didn't do anything else. I went to acting class, I spent all my money on acting class. And you know, stole food from [the] restaurant, and didn't spend any money.

And when you went in to read for Northern Exposure, did they give you the pilot script?

Actually [they] didn't, because in the pilot script I didn't say anything. In the pilot script Shelly was an Indian, in the original script.

I mean, obviously it changed when they cast me. I wasn't supposed to be an Indian. But for my audition, I read two scenes from the fourth and fifth scripts, where Shelly actually starts doing things. But the first three scripts, I had no idea what my character was going to be like, because I didn't do anything.

What's the difference between Cynthia Geary and Shelly?

As far as my background, it's completely different. Shelly grew up in a broken home and really had no parental supervision, and left at eighteen with this older man. And I grew up in a really structured family.

I'm the youngest of four children and my parents are still married, and they're still very involved with everything I'm doing, and they advise me on everything. And I went to college and graduated from college.

What kind of advice do you get from your folks?

What do they tell me now? Um, they give me really good advice, because they're not over-whelmed by the TV industry, so their advice is really practical. My father's a money manager and a stock broker. [His advice was] to invest my money and not to spend all my money and to save it.

And my mother's given me some great advice about enjoying my life and not getting too busy, where I forget to feed my soul. I got this great letter from her [during] last season's hiatus, because I worked all during hiatus—I did another movie—and I didn't ever take a break.

And she said, Make sure you don't burn out, and do things you enjoy. So you go to hear music, because I'm a music major, and you sing and you take voice lessons, and you go to the mountains and you walk around. And [you] don't get so all-consumed with it that you forget to enjoy your life.

Is it tough advice to take? I mean it tends to take you over.

It does, if you let it. But I think that I've been really lucky in the fact that I have such a stable upbringing, my family's really stable....I mean I love this, it's a great job, and I really appreciate it. But I think I appreciate it for what it is.... I don't think that I'm Shelly. I mean, I don't expect everybody, when we get off the set, to wait on me like they do on the set.

That's a refreshing attitude in acting.

Well, maybe it's because I'm new. But I do think it has a lot to do with my family. And my boyfriend's not in the business. He's got his feet on the ground, and he's really down to earth.

What does he do?

Real-estate development.

Is he a Seattle person?

No, he's from L.A., but he just moved, he moved here.

And do you stay here in Seattle, do you have a house here?

I just bought a house, a month ago.

As soon as they picked up the fifty episodes?

Yeah.

Everybody in the cast and crew have done that.

I think I started it. I was the first one. But I come from, I mean I grew up watching *Wall Street Week* and all this stuff with my dad, and so I looked for my house. I had been looking for a year, just as a hobby... on weekends and stuff, so I knew what I wanted and I found a great deal... on my birthday actually.

What's your birthday?

March 21st.

So now the show's a monster hit. Do you realize how big a hit it is?

Yeah, but maybe not. Because on purpose I think I'm a little bit oblivious to it. I go out with my friends and my family and visitors, and they always notice that people are recognizing me, and I don't. And I don't know if that's on purpose or not, but I don't ever really notice anybody unless they come up to me and say, "Hi, I love your show."

And I think that's maybe a defense mechanism, because you don't want to be paranoid and think everybody's staring at you all the time.

You look very young. You'll be playing teens for the next twenty years.

Yeah, I'm really lucky because I look young.

Why is that? Does your family look young?

Yeah, my family looks really young.... Maybe one of the reasons is because I grew up in the south and the weather is really conducive to good skin. It's so humid, and it's so hot, and my mother's really big on sunscreen.

My mother's is beautiful, and looks, you know she's sixty-one and she looks fifty.

So it's going to be the same way for you.

Yeah. And all the kids in our family look really young for their age.

How have things changed for you since the show began? Have your ambitions changed?

No, not really. I mean, I always wanted to be an actress when growing up, from a really young age.

I knew I wanted to be in entertainment, I thought I wanted to be a singer. My mother is a music teacher, and I ended up getting into acting

because I wasn't so sure that I had the voice to really make it as a singer....But I don't think my goals have really changed. I'd like to be married, and someday I think I'd like kids, I mean no time soon. But I'd like to be in feature film.

Is the reality of show business what you expected it to be?

It's a lot better. It's *much* more fun. It's still really amazing to me that I get paid for what I do, and have such a great life for somebody my age...

For somebody my age I make a lot of money, or of any age really, and to own a house, and to live in such a beautiful place, and to have fun at work everyday. I mean, it's *great*. And we get treated great. You get treated like royalty. And you get free stuff. I mean, Reebok calls you and wants you to wear their clothes, so you get all this free stuff. I mean, it's fun.

What would you like to see Shelly doing?

The main thing I want to see happen is, I want to see Shelly be more involved with more characters other than Holling. Not that I don't love John Cullum, he's an incredible actor.

I think they've really developed Holling and Shelly's relationship and they've done so many wonderful things with it, but I'd like to get involved with the other characters more, because they haven't involved my story line as much with some of the other characters.

I'd like to see me get involved with Maggie, and Ruth-Anne, and the way I relate to women, and Ed....Maggie and I have this kind of, you know, it's completely two different levels, I say one thing, she says [another], and we never hear each other. It's a funny relationship.

But it's very funny, because this is the first time I've been in Roslyn since we started shooting, because my character never goes outside. I'm always in the studio, in the bar. I shouldn't say

that, because I'm going to say this too much and I'm going to be out in the middle of the freezing cold, all the time, outside. But I would like to see her get more involved with the other people in the town.

Of all the episodes, do you have a favorite moment?

Yeah. My favorite scene that I've done—oh God, this is hard, because there are a lot of shows I really like. My favorite scene is when I'm yelling at Holling about my big feet; there's this show where he asks me to marry him because he sees that I have big feet.

As an actress, I just really liked that scene because it went from bright, being happy, to the next thing, like, "*What* are you talking about? What's wrong? Hey, wait a minute, you just stepped on something, you just said something that I'm really sensitive about," to being really angry, to being hurt and mad. And I got to go through the whole arc and they didn't cut anything.

And so, that's my favorite scene from the acting standpoint. Show-wise, my favorite show, I really didn't do anything in, but [it] was the show where we flung the piano, and Maggie's house burned down...

I'm guessing that you have lots of fan mail. Is it friendly, marriage proposals? Are there people writing you saying, "You little tart, how dare you take up with an older man?"

No! And I'm really surprised, because I haven't gotten any negative response. Really, no negative response. I've gotten a few really weird ones, but not many. I mean most of them are really nice. And they all say, "I love your character, I love your show...you're my favorite character, please send me a picture." They *all* ask for pictures...

They made up the story because I was on *Arsenio Hall*, and to make a long story short, he asked me if I was serious about my boyfriend, and if I wanted to marry him. And I said yes. And he said, "Well, why don't you propose to him on TV?" And I said, "Well, I don't want to do that, I want him to ask *me*." And he got down on his knees and proposed to my boyfriend on TV for me.

So anyway, they made this big story about how my boyfriend said no, and I'm thirty and I'm desperate.

Oh, I have gotten one negative thing. I found out I was in the tabloids last weekend, and they said I was thirty and desperate. First of all, I'm not thirty, and I'm not desperate.

How does your boyfriend react to all this?

He takes it wonderfully. He grew up in Malibu, and he's kind of used to the business. He thought it was great...

After Dan Quayle took on Murphy Brown, I thought Shelly and Holling would be next.

I know, it's amazing...[but] the reason why Holling and Shelly, why I don't get any negative press, is because their relationship is handled so well.

They're very loving and they care about each other, and it doesn't seem weird, or it's not gross.

ELAINE MILES

(MARILYN WHIRLWIND)

Elaine Miles had to be convinced to become Marilyn Whirlwind, Dr. Joel's sage and subtle assistant, and even now she's not completely certain it's all been worth it.

Told a visiting writer wants to talk to her before he leaves town, she graciously drives over to the soundstage—in her shiny, new, blue cabin-and-a-half pick-up truck—on her day off and proceeds to answer the visitor's questions with complete forthrightness.

Unlike Marilyn, says Elaine, she's emotional. She laughs easily, but, when she thinks of her late father, a few tears flow as well.

How Elaine Miles became Marilyn Whirlwind is, by now, a famous story: Elaine, who had no intention of becoming an actress, accompanied her mother to the audition and then had to be convinced to read for the part. Not only was she hired to play Marilyn, and went on to become a regular, but her mother also has appeared on the show.

She remembers waiting for her mom at the audition and how John Vreeke—an aspiring Seattle-area theatrical director who had then just been hired to find Native American and other extras for the *Northern Exposure* pilot, and who has since become the assistant to the producers— "was there typing, and he kept looking at me. He gradually talked me into auditioning."

What did John Vreeke do to finally convince you to audition?

Oh, he'd just type and then he'd go into the other room. My mom was in the other room...and then he'd come out and start talking to me again, and telling how much fun it would be just to *try*, and actually I was just getting cranky and hot. It was hot that day...

What were you doing beforehand?

Nothing. Absolutely nothing. Traveling. We used to go to powwows all over the United States.

Really? What did you do at these powwows?

Dance. Because both my mom and I used to dance.

And you would make a living at that?

Well, yeah, I guess. Well, dad worked for Boeing, and he retired a couple years ago. He passed away in November [1991]. He got to work with us on the show, too, as background.

Your mother had a part, too.

She's had a couple of parts. She's been Mrs. Anku [Ed's aunt] the very first season, and then just this past season she was Marilyn's mother. So that worked out good.

They wanted my dad, too, cause, you know that scene that was going to be all Marilyn and her parents?

They wanted my real parents. But my dad said two stars in the family was good enough.

How did your mother take not getting the part?

Oh, she took it very well. Both of us, we didn't even think either one of us would get the part, cause we were both just excited after we auditioned. And then mom says, "Well, if we don't get it, at least we can be extras and make fifty bucks a day doing nothing." And then I go, "Yeah, and then we can meet all those movie stars."...So, we were just excited about being offered to be extras.

And how long did it take you to find out that you got the part?

Well, I auditioned on Saturday, and [they] called us back Sunday evening to tell us we had to be at the studio to audition in front of the director and the producers. That was on Monday afternoon. We went back up there and there [were] four of us. My mom and I and two other women. Then, afterwards, they told me that I got the part and I started to work on it Wednesday.

Were you thrilled when you got the part?

I screamed....Because they took both of us and [they] said, "Elaine, you got the part of Marilyn, and momma comes with us because [we] liked the mother-daughter team, and [we're] going to write her in as Marilyn's mother."

What's the difference between Marilyn and Elaine?

Marilyn is very easygoing, very calm. She knows what she's going to do. And me, I'm like a total basketcase all the time. I *never* know what I'm going to do.

Now, it seems like I'm always rushing to do this, rushing to do that. Working here, it's like hurry, hurry, hurry; and wait, wait, wait.

Is it the way you thought it would be?

I never in my whole life dreamt I'd be doing this, *never*. I used to be the couch potato. I always watched *All My Children, General Hospital*...Oh, yeah, my favorite was *Knots Landing*, I used to *always* watch *Knots Landing*.

When you were watching Knots Landing, did you ever think of the lives that the actors led?

No. I used to just watch it for the characters.

Do you think it's worth it? Are you having fun?

Oh, there's some episodes where I have fun doing it. And then there are some episodes where I just really don't want to come in, but, I have to. I have a contract.

Well, you could always break it.

Yeah. I almost did that once.

Why?

Well, that was when my father passed away, and it seemed like the whole world was against me, and I just wanted to be off, and go back to my old self again.

What happens to you on the streets?

Oh, God. I can't even walk down the streets. I used to love going to rodeos, and I can't even go to a rodeo, the people recognize me.

It wouldn't be so bad if they would just say hello, and then just go from there. But some people [have] got to stop and tell me their whole life story. I don't mind that, but it's like when I'm watching rodeo and enjoying it, and then you miss seeing what happens.

I come from a rodeo family. My mother used to be a jockey. She used to team up with my uncles, in the old days.

And do you ride as well?

I ride horses. But I'm not...really into it like she was. If we stayed on the reservation, I'd probably be really into it. Because you know, we had our horses right there...

That's the downside of it. What's the upside?

The upside? The money. I have money to

spend. If I want something I can just go buy it. I have *excellent* credit.

Now, I actually have credit. I have American Express. I bought my furniture on credit and I paid it all off already....And then I have a banking and a savings [account]...

Did you buy anything that you really wanted? Have you moved?

Yeah, I moved out of my parents' home. I used to live with my parents, but now I have my own place. So it's nice.

Will you keep doing this?

Ah, when they asked me that like the second season I said, "Oh, I'm not really sure, I don't know." But now if you ask me, I think I *do*, I think I want to pursue this. And hopefully, I'll get offers from movies and stuff.

What do you think it is that people love about Marilyn, or about you?

Her quiet subtle ways. She knows what's going to happen before everybody else does.

What do you think about the ways that Native Americans are portrayed on the show?

I think they are portrayed fine. I have no problems with that. I'm happy they're actually using real Native Americans, even as background. That's important, too. They've done a lot more with the Native Americans.

Do you have a favorite moment or a favorite episode?

My favorite episode was when Marilyn takes over the office...when Joel and Maggie went to Juneau. And Marilyn kind of took over the office

and told the guy he was going to die, when he didn't quit smoking. That was pretty funny.

If you were writing the show, what would you have Marilyn do that she hasn't done yet?

Oh, well, Marilyn has done just about everything. She's gone into business with Maurice, with ostriches of all things. That was another of my favorites, cause I got to work with Barry.

But the one thing I want for Marilyn is for her to have a Native American boyfriend.

For the first several episodes, Marilyn wasn't listed as a regular cast member...

Right, for the first eight episodes she was a guest star. And then after that, I'm a regular [in] that second season.

I'm the only one [in the credits] that says "Elaine Miles as Marilyn." They list my character *and* my name...so I don't mind that.

You know, people were telling me, You should be up there with the rest of them. And I go, Well I don't mind *that*, because I have my character name and my real name, so people know me as Elaine Miles.

DARREN E. BURROWS
(ED CHIGLIAK)

Darren Burrows pronounces himself just a kid from Kansas and professes to be bemused by sudden success.

On set and out on location, he whoops it up between takes, playfully throwing air punches and trading good-ol'-boy barbs with the grips. But when the camera rolls, the Kansas Kid is completely professional and totally Ed.

Later, when he flirtatiously tells a wardrobe girl how pretty she looks, she just gives him an indulgent, affectionate there-he-goes-again smile.

At first, he's wary of the stranger hanging out with the cast and crew, and an A.D. (assistant director) passes the word that it would be best to not even approach him until after he's done his scenes. Eventually, though, he invites the visitor to his trailer, and they kick back and rap.

How did you get the gig?

It was just one of many auditions where you go, oh God. You know, in the beginning I couldn't get hired for TV to save my soul to tell you the truth. And so for me, I had already done like four films....

You were excellent in Casualties of War.

Oh, no way, really? Funny thing is I spent three months over there for that...in Thailand. And for me it was just, like, okay this is when everything going on with the film slows down, to make room for pilot season. And anything you go up for, you're guaranteed about twenty-four actual hours [of work]. An hour a day. A bunch of time wasted, really.

When I read the script, I fell in love with it and I thought it was great. But I didn't think [it would go].

What's the difference between Ed and Darren? And what does Darren bring to Ed that's not on the page?

Ahh. I bring everything but my clothes and the words. Obviously, I'm basically a hired hand, in that [they say] "Here, you'll say this." And so, that's what I'll say. But Ed's kind of—I don't know if it's because I've been doing it for so long or what—he's almost metamorphosized into an entity of his own, where they could really hand Ed the phone book to read, or the dictionary, and it would be Ed reading it.

As far as the other part, Ed to me, the beautiful thing about Ed is, to me he's kind of like the child within us all—oh God, I don't know, it's kind of corny, but it's really pretty Zen-like, I would think.

Did anybody instruct you on how to play the part?

No, I just kind of, here's my theory: you know, if you go into an audition, or go in and try to get any type of job really, and try to figure out what they want: Okay, what are they looking for?

Even if you get lucky enough to figure it out, then every day, every time you show up for that job, you're going to be going crazy, going "What do they want today? Oh, my God," you know?

And you're probably not able to figure it out, just because I think a lot of times people don't really know what they want.

They have an idea, but it's more, it's like when I'm shopping for clothes I don't really know what I want, but when I see it, then I go, "That's it, that's what I've been looking for all day."

And so, I just kind of go in and do it the way that I would like to do, or the way that feels best to me, or, well, in my case basically the only way I

can do it. And then if I do get the job, I can pretty much have a heck of a good time doing it, and less all the headaches.

They say that great acting isn't acting, it's reacting. The cut-aways to you, when you're between the words, during the silences, those gestures and when you start to say something, and then say something else, where did that come from?

I think if you just listen. I don't think most people listen or pay attention in real life that much. They're mostly doing their own thing and not really aware of what's going on around them. Especially when you're doing a scene, or acting, and you've already read the words and played out the conversation a couple of times, then there really is no listening required. And I think, if you *just listen*.

You see, I'm not like most people here, like a lot of people, like, Rob Morrow is a trained actor in the theater and the arts, and knows about the history. See, I don't really know that much about that.

I just kind of, it's kind of like acting by Wednesday for me. What did Cagney say? "Plant both feet on the ground and look the other actor in the eye and tell the truth." And if you are operating from the truth, then, yeah. I don't know, this is getting pretty esoteric, but somewhere in there lies my truth.

What are you going to do on hiatus?

[*Large laugh*] I'm not sure I want to talk about it....[This year] I rode all over the country on my bike....I've wanted one since I was twelve, and God's blessed me enough that now I can have one, and so I do. Yeah, I rode seven thousand miles, all over the south of the country...

How do you think the show got to be such a success?

In the beginning, the only thing the show had going for it, the main selling point was, it was the only original series on the air. And everything else was reruns. And there was no pilot done.

So once they cast it, and sent us all up here, they kind of just let us all run wild.

Josh Brand directed the first show, but once that was over we really never saw or talked to anybody. It was a done deal, eight episodes and we were out of there, and nobody counted on, I don't even know of a contingency plan that they had for coming back. And then, when we got all the fan mail....

So, when we did [come back on air], they didn't have scripts, nobody was ready....

That kind of allowed us, that whole first season, allowed *us* to set the pace. You got people like John Cullum, who's like this humungous Broadway star.

...He is definitely the nicest man on the show, nicer than me. Barry Corbin has done like hundreds of films. He's like an old pro.

So you know, I did my thing, but basically just stood back and watched all this going on. And it's like they've developed their whole thing to a point where there's a lot of scenes where characters just pass through a scene, and not much goes on.

You could make, like, a whole show about like John Cullum's character, for instance. But then, at the same time, then when he's just passing through a scene he brings all that weight, that whole world, through the scene with him. So, it's not just, like, "passing through a scene."

Peg Phillips is so wonderful to work with, we have a great time working together, and for me that's the real fun of the show....We get, like, that spontaneity thing going. Cause she listens.

Because a lot of times when you work with actors, who, when they have it all planned out

ahead of time, what this means and that means, if you were to say a wrong line...then there wouldn't be an appropriate response. The other response would come and it wouldn't make sense.

Is success what you thought it would be?

To me, success is everything I was ever told it would be, except that a lot of people have the misconception that it guarantees you a trouble-free life, where there's no problems and that.

The reality of my situation is, I can only eat so much food, and I really don't like escargot and such. And so, for me it's mashed potatoes and gravy, and nobody's there to mash them for me, really. And if your car breaks down on the freeway, you're still really bumming....

You're a single man in the nineties?

Yeah. Yeah. But [Fame], it's let me have my motorcycle, it's let me have my El Camino out there, but, you know, you don't want to have more than one beer anywhere.

See, Hollywood really isn't my life. Although it's not like I haven't worked hard for where I am, and haven't eaten my share of ketchup/mustard sandwiches. I ran away from home when I was sixteen and went to L.A., and I guess the last four years have been good.

Kansas, right?

Yeah.

By the way, is your official bio true?

You know what? I'm not really a half Indian. I'm probably about an eighth, or a little less. And my hair is dyed.

I'm not really sure, it's kind of like when you're a kid and your parents say to you, "Hey you know, you've got some German blood in you." And you think about that for a minute, maybe about World War Two or an old war movie you saw, and then, okay, you're back on the jungle gym. And that's how it kind of was for me.

I never really got that interested in it until I started doing this show. And at that point, my grandparents had passed on, and I've probably learned more about what little part of me is that from the show.

Just from Elaine Miles and her mother. [They] really took me under their wing and introduced me [around].

What color is your real hair?

Dish-water blond. Had a few dishes washed in it.

After Northern Exposure *runs its course, what do you want to do?*

I'd like to do a picture or two a year, and go into cattle ranching.

PEG PHILLIPS
(RUTH-ANNE MILLER)

If possible, actress Peggy Phillips cuts an even more formidable, heroic figure in person than her character, Ruth-Anne, proprietor of the Cicely, Alaska, general store, does on screen.

After all, this is not just any seventy-four-year-old actress. This is the woman who was a navy wife, lived all around the country, divorced, worked forty years as an accountant, raised four children alone, *then*—at sixty-five—went to college to pursue her lifelong acting dream.

This is the same woman who founded and still directs a drama workshop program at Echo Glen Children's Center, a correctional facility for children who have committed major crimes.

One late Roslyn afternoon, after finishing an exterior scene on main street, she walks the block-and-a-half to her mobile home with a visitor, disdaining the van waiting to chauffeur her, and stopping to chat with each of the beaming tourists who ask to have a snapshot of themselves with Ruth-Anne.

I don't know much about your background.

Oh, well gosh, everybody does....

Well, I'm seventy-four, and I wanted to act all my life, but I was a Depression kid and didn't get to go to school. Got married, had kids, finally ended up with a big family, raising them by myself...mostly in Northern California.

I was born and raised here, but then I migrated when I was about twenty....

I worked in San Francisco and lived in Marin County, and I did community theater then. I never lost my desire to act, but I wanted some training. So I got the kids raised, and they went up and went to college and had *their* kids, and I helped raise the grandkids.

And when I was sixty-five, I retired from my work that I earned a living by, and enrolled in the University of Washington in the drama school.

What was your job?

I was an accountant during the daytime and an actor at night. And anyway, I hadn't gotten my degree yet, because I went to work too soon. I did all my course work at the drama school, and then took some advanced [classes] at a local acting school. In my freshman year I got an agent and went to work. Doing commercials and films. I've done seven films now....

How did you get the role in Northern Exposure?

Well, I should have through my agent, but I didn't. My agent didn't send me out for this. I think she misunderstood.

As you can tell, I never did get roles for what I call "cookie-jar grandmothers"—little, sweet, aproned grandmothers in the kitchen. They just don't give me those roles.

I did a lot of bag ladies, witches, you know. But anyway I didn't get called for the first audition, but the producers of *Northern Exposure* didn't find the person they wanted for this role, so on callbacks, they called the casting director here...and she knew my work...and she sent me. And I got it, just like that.

Ruth-Anne was initially a guest, she wasn't a regular. Tell me when you learned that you were going to be a regular character.

It just evolved.... The first eight [episodes], I was in all but three of those. But I was just a bit player, I had no background, no history, I had no

relationship to anybody. I was kind of a plot device. So finally, toward the end of the second eight, [it changed]. I did sixteen episodes, most of them standing behind that counter just letting people say things at me. But I was lucky to have the work, you know. I was a day player. I didn't crab.

But, at the same time, I was working with my acting coach on how in the world do you play "atmosphere?" He didn't know.

So I sat down and wrote like we did in acting school, a biography of Ruth-Anne, from the time she was born to the present day. And then I wrote a little precis [on] what I think Ruth-Anne's relationships really are with the people in town. And I sent that to Josh Brand and John Falsey, and lo and behold, the first episode last fall—the one where Maggie gets drunk after Rick is dead, and I put her to bed—they gave me that long monologue, talking about my husband, about my affair with an RAF pilot. They started right in there. Then they started giving me some background.

Was that from your biography?

No. No, I didn't put that in my biography. I had myself born in Idaho, they put me in Portland. But, nonetheless, they started in.

My relationships with people they accepted. Now, for instance, my relationship with Ed. I said in my little thing, when he was a little boy, he was an orphan. And he hung around town and most of the townspeople didn't like him, but I did. I just loved him. And I'd send him on errands from the store and slip him fifty cents.

Lo and behold, they started writing Ed into my store. They had me hire him.

What is it about you or Ruth-Anne that catches the imagination?

I don't know. I do get a lot of fan letters.

What do they say?

They say that I'm an inspiration. Of course, part of it is my personal life.

When I got my drama training about five years ago, I started drama workshops at the children's prison here. In Snoqualmie....Echo Glen's Children Center it's called. They featured it on *Entertainment Tonight*....

[We do] fast moving improvs, mimes. We don't do script work, because a lot of them can't read, and they are kids from ten to twenty. Anyway, I put the arm on a lot of theater professionals here in town—directors, actors—and they teach, volunteer. It's been great.

But since that's been featured, I get a lot of fan mail about my personal life, too. But the thing that people see in Ruth-Anne—it's funny, I don't

see Ruth-Anne that way that much—is her wisdom, her ability to bring people together.

Some people see her, even younger people see her, as the person who settles difficulties and keeps the place going on an even keel. I don't see her that way particularly. I see her as an internal character.

What do you mean by "internal?"

A woman with her own life. She had grown children, two boys, and she has her store and relationships with people, and she's very intensely personal in her relationships. I don't think she sees herself as the matriarch of the town at all, or thinks she's particularly wise.

She just knows what she thinks is right and what she thinks is wrong. At her age, she's not going to put up with anything that she thinks is wrong.

How are you different than her?

I'm afraid there isn't too much difference. This is an actor's dream they've given me. They've given me wonderful scenes and wonderful dialogue, and turned me loose with it and let me just build this character.

Do you have a favorite moment?

Yes. Heavens, yes. When I danced on my grave....

It was a wonderful experience, and that's my favorite. Darren and I both, we *loved* that particular one. We just felt so at home with it, and each other. It's where he finds out I'm seventy-five and he's so scared I'm going to die, he gives me the birthday [present]. And then we go up.

And I danced for four hours on that mountain top, at seventy-four years old....

I read that script, and just said, "Thank the good Lord I'm in this."

You raised a family and then returned to acting. Do you have any regrets about the choices you've made?

No. I enjoyed every single minute of my life, and it's all evolved. And I hit acting at just the right time for me, apparently. I have no regrets....As far as the way my life has gone, I take you to mean, Do I think I've been held back by circumstance? No way. I enjoyed my kids, I had four of them. I enjoy my grandkids, and I have four of them.

What's the age range of your children?

My oldest child is fifty, and my youngest great-grandchild is four. So, I've got them all down the line.

Does the four-year-old ever get to see the show?

Oh, sure. But they live in Australia, so they didn't see it until they came over here. And they came on the set, and their mother and dad acted as extras.

The actors here run the gamut in age and experience, and some have gone from nothing to huge success. Do you ever look at them and think, if only you were a few years older, you would know how to handle it better?

Yes, I think that. Particularly about one of them. No, I think it's very tough on a young person, particularly someone who has not had to struggle. Now, some of our young people really had to struggle in the acting game, and they understand. But the young people [who] don't [understand], they surprise me, they amaze me, they take it for granted a lot. And it really upsets me. And I just keep pounding away at it.

One of them said to me, "The producers make more than actors." And I said, "Alright, you're nobody's fool, you took up acting and you knew producers made more. Why didn't you become a producer? You wanted to act, and you're making damn good money, not only good money, but a lot of it." More than they ever thought they were going to make. Steady. For years! *God.*

It's too bad. Now Barry Corbin, he's been around so long, he's got his feet planted, solid on the ground. John Cullum, who is sixty-four, and he's won two Tonys—I mean, he's a famous man; the most diffident and darling man—and he says fame is fleeting. Every job he's ever had for the last forty years, he knows is going to be his last. Because sometimes it is.

Is there something you would like Ruth-Anne to be doing that she hasn't done?

No. I talked to Josh and suggested several things, and they've done them all.

Really? What did you suggest?

I suggested that I play with Ed, and they did, they gave us two wonderful episodes. I suggested at the wrap party last year to Josh, that Maurice and I have a fight, because Maurice and I are far apart—I'm a liberal and he's a conservative....

The one I objected to, but it turned out fine...[was] about a younger man that I know, that's known in the town, [who] comes back to town—he's a salesman of clothes—and falls in love with Ruth-Anne.

And I have a thing about old women and younger men, personally, and I said to Josh that I didn't want to do that. And he said, "It will be alright." And I said, "Are you sure? Is it tastefully written?"

And he said yes, and it was. Very, very sweetly, tenderly written. And of course she turns him down, and it has some overtones. But it was a lovely episode.

As the old saying goes, *there are lies, damn lies and statistics.* As a general rule, and as any reporter on the entertainment beat can tell you, actors' official biographies—corporate and anonymously written—may be safely added to this list.

Happily, however, the *Northern Exposure* biographies are, generally, exceptions to this rule. A recent, unscientific survey of the actors, who in some cases hadn't even *seen* their own bios, turned up only one egregious error.

"I'm not really a half Indian," said actor Darren Burrows, who plays Ed Chigliak, Cicely's resident cineaste. "I'm probably about an eighth or a little less." All the official bios follow.

Rob Morrow

Rob Morrow portrays Dr. Joel Fleischman, the quintessential "fish out of water" in MCA Television's critically-acclaimed CBS series *Northern Exposure*. Joel is an inveterate New Yorker who has been reluctantly transplanted to the remote Alaskan town of Cicely. Immediately welcomed by the oddball locals of Cicely, the reluctant Joel struggles to operate in the sparse, makeshift medical office set up for him and has trouble accepting what passes for "normal" behavior in this eccentric little town. But Morrow brings a disarming warmth to Joel's griping as he copes with his perpetual relocation angst.

Born and raised in New Rochelle, N.Y., Morrow began pursuing a professional acting career fresh out of high school. A number of odd jobs in the theater led to his first break. While working as an assistant to Michael Bennett on *Dream Girls,* Bennett cast him for a major role in the play *Third Street* at the Circle Repertory Theater.

Among Morrow's more than thirty-five performances on stage are leading roles in Chaim Potok's musical adaptation of *The Chosen,* Michael Bennett's *Scandal, Soulful Scream of the Chosen Son, The Boys of Winter* and *Slam.* His most recent theatrical performance was in the Naked Angels and subsequent Long Wharf productions of Jon Robin Baitz's *The Substance of Fire.*

Morrow made his film debut in 1986 in the comedy *Private Resort* with Johnny Depp. In addition to his leading role on the television series

Tattingers, Morrow guest starred in the series *Fame* and *Spencer: For Hire.*

Morrow maintains his residence in New York City where he is a member of the Ensemble Studio Theater and the New York Stage and Film Company. In his spare time, he has developed a new and unlikely obsession—golf—a sport he grudgingly learned in order to realistically portray the golf-obsessed Dr. Fleischman.

Janine Turner

Janine Turner portrays Maggie O'Connell, a beautiful, independent bush pilot and landlady. As Dr. Joel Fleischman's (Rob Morrow) primary nemesis, Maggie struggles between her disdain for Joel's whiny ways and her reluctant physical attraction to him.

Turner was nominated for Best Actress, Quality Drama by the Viewers for Quality Television in 1991.

Born in Lincoln, Nebraska, and raised in Fort Worth, Texas, Turner began her performing career with modeling and dance at the age of three. Beginning with a dance apprenticeship with the Fort Worth Ballet in her preteen years, she moved easily into acting with a performance in a local theater production of *Charlotte's Web.* At fifteen, her mother took her portfolio to the Wilhelmina modeling agency and two weeks later she became their youngest client. After studying at the Professional Children's School while in New York, Turner and her parents returned to Texas.

Back in Fort Worth, Turner was discovered by Leonard Katzman, producer of *Dallas,* and was cast in a recurring role as Lucy's friend Susan. Encouraged by Katzman, Turner moved to Los Angeles after high school where she landed her first series, a late-night soap *Behind the Screen,* written by David Jacobs of *Knots Landing* fame. Although the series lasted only thirteen weeks, it drew the attention of the producers of *General Hospital,* who subsequently signed her to a year-long contract. During this time she did a cameo in the feature film *Young Doctors in Love,* costarred in *Knights of the City,* and portrayed Shevan Tillman in Dino De Laurentiis' feature film *Tai-Pan.*

Turner moved back to New York in 1986 to further hone her acting skills. She spent the next three years studying with Marcia Haufrecht (a member of Lee Strasberg's Actors Studio) and acting coach Mira Rastova. She went on to perform in several Off-Broadway productions such as *Full Moon and High Tide in the Ladies Room* with the Ensemble Studio Theatre. When in NYC, Turner is also a member of the avant-garde theatre group, "The Common Ground Theatre," where only original works are performed.

Her additional film credits include costarring roles in George Romero's *Monkey Shines, Steel Magnolias* as Olympia Dukakis's niece, Nancy Beth Marlmilion, and *The Ambulance* with Eric Roberts and James Earl Jones.

Turner resides near Seattle, Washington, and maintains a residence in Texas. She enjoys horseback riding (on her horse, Maggie), writing poetry, attending the opera and ballet and listening to classical and, naturally, country music. She is not often found without her traveling companion of ten years, her dog, Eclaire.

John Corbett

John Corbett portrays Chris Stevens, Cicely's resident disc jockey. Known to quote Walt Whitman over the air on KBHR's "Chris-in-the-Morning" show, as well as playing an off-the-wall musical mix ranging from jazz to show tunes to rock 'n' roll, Chris provides a running commentary on the offbeat goings-on in Cicely, Alaska.

Born on May 9 in Virginia, Corbett grew up in the sixties, a free-thinking liberal in middle class surroundings. Unclear about a future career path, Corbett spent six years working in a steel factory until an injury forced him to redirect himself. After enrolling in a local junior college, he discovered the drama department, and captivated, committed himself to a full-time acting career.

Shortly after he moved to Los Angeles, his professional career began with a series of high profile television commercials for companies such as Samsung Electronics, Foster's Beer, and DHL Courier. After appearing in over fifty national commercials, Corbett won a guest-starring role on the highly-acclaimed ABC series "Wonder Years."

Corbett made his motion picture debut in *Flight of the Intruder* with Danny Glover and Willem Dafoe for Paramount Pictures. He has also appeared in stage productions of *Witness for the Prosecution, Hair, Under Milkwood,* and *Marathon '33.*

Corbett currently resides near Seattle, Washington, and in Los Angeles, California, where he plays percussion in The Matthew Stoneman Band, a jazz-influenced New Age musical group. In addition to his musical pursuits, Corbett enjoys playing softball, basketball, and shooting pool.

Barry Corbin

Barry Corbin portrays Maurice Minnifield, town patriarch of Cicely, Alaska.

A burly ex-astronaut and gung-ho president of the Cicely Chamber of Commerce, Maurice sees Cicely as a haven of limitless potential, soon to be the new "Alaskan Riviera." He also feels it is his duty to keep Dr. Fleischman (Rob Morrow) practicing in Cicely to secure the town's future urbanization.

Born and raised in Dawson County, Texas, Corbin has appeared in almost one hundred films and television shows in the last decade. He began his performing career at Texas Tech, where he studied and performed everything from the great masters to contemporary playwrights.

After two years in the Marines, Corbin began performing in regional theater across the country for three years. He moved to New York in 1964, and during the next decade starred on Broadway, Off Broadway, and in regional and dinner theaters in such roles as Henry in *Henry V,* Jud in *Oklahoma,* Oscar in *The Odd Couple,* Falstaff in *The Merry Wives of Windsor,* Henry in *Becket,* and Macbeth in *Macbeth.*

Corbin relocated to Los Angeles in 1977 and was writing plays for National Public Radio when he was cast as Uncle Bob in the feature film *Urban Cowboy.* He has also created memorable performances in films such as *The Man Who Loved Women, Nothing in Common, War Games, Best Little Whorehouse in Texas,* and *Honky-Tonk Man.* Corbin also had a featured role in the John Hughes film *Career Opportunities.*

Corbin's television credits include numerous miniseries and telefilms such as *Lonesome Dove, The Thorn Birds, Fatal Vision, A Death in California, Last Flight Out, Young Harry Houdini,* and *Bitter Harvest.* He also starred in *The Chase* and

The Keys, as well as the TNT Western *Conagher,* with Sam Elliott and Katharine Ross. Corbin has guest starred on more than a dozen series including *Hill Street Blues, Call to Glory, Matlock* and *Murder She Wrote.* He also starred in the series *Boone, Spies,* and Showtime's *Washingtoon.* In addition to his impressive acting resume, Corbin is on the faculty of Texas Tech and is a published playwright, having had seven radio plays performed on the Pacifica Radio Network. An avid horseman, he competes in celebrity rodeos around the country. Corbin resides with his wife and two sons in the Los Angeles area.

John Cullum

Tony Award-winning stage actor John Cullum portrays Holling Vincoeur, a sixty-two-year-old naturalist and adventurer. Holling has given up his big game hunting days to settle down as proprietor of Cicely's local tavern. Holling has also settled into domestic bliss with his eighteen-year-old girlfriend, Shelly Tambo (Cynthia Geary), a former Miss Northwest Passage, who was brought to Cicely by Holling's best friend, Maurice Minnifield (Barry Corbin).

Born and raised in Knoxville, Tennessee, Cullum majored in Speech and English at the University of Tennessee before fulfilling his obligation as an army reserve officer by serving two years in Korea. On his return, he relocated to New York to pursue a professional stage career.

In his first Broadway show, Cullum originated the role of Sir Dinidan and acted as a standby for Richard Burton in the Broadway production of *Camelot*. He received the Theatre World Award and a Tony nomination for his first starring role in *On a Clear Day You Can See Forever*. In 1975, he was honored with his first Tony Award for Best Actor in a Musical for *Shenandoah* as well as the Drama Desk Award and the Outer Circles Critics Awards. He received a second Tony in 1978 for *On the Twentieth Century*.

Cullum has also starred on Broadway in the role of Laertes in Richard Burton's *Hamlet*, directed by Sir John Gielgud, *Deathtrap*, *Private Lives*, with Richard Burton and Elizabeth Taylor, *Doubles*, *Man of La Mancha*, and the musical *1776* as Rutledge, a role he re-created on screen. Most recently, Cullum starred in Andrew Lloyd Webber's production of *Aspects of Love* with Sarah Brightman. He is also involved with numerous other performing companies including Joseph Papp's Shakespeare in the Park, the Los Angeles Civic Light Opera and the Pabst Theater of Milwaukee.

Cullum relocated to Los Angeles for a starring role in Dennis Weaver's series *Buck James* and more recently guest starred in and directed episodes on NBC's *Quantum Leap*. He starred in television's highest rated movie, *The Day After* for ABC, as well as *Shootdown* starring Angela Lansbury. On PBS, he starred in *Summer*, from the Edith Wharton series and portrayed the great American poet Carl Sandburg in *Echoes & Syllables* in the "Great Performances" series, and is a spokesman on the Arts & Entertainment channel for "Victorian Days."

His feature film credits include *Sweet Country* with Jane Alexander, *Marie* with Sissy Spacek, *The Prodigal* with Hope Lange, and the film *1776*.

Cullum and his wife, Emily Frankel, an international renowned dancer as well as playwright and novelist, currently reside in Bellevue, Washington, and also maintain residences in New York City and Malibu, California.

Cynthia Geary

Cynthia Geary portrays Shelly Tambo, an eighteen-year-old former Miss Northwest Passage. After arriving in Cicely with Maurice Minnifield (Barry Corbin), who performed judging duties at the Miss Northwest Passage pageant, Shelly quickly dumped him for his best friend, sixty-two-year-old Holling Vincoeur (John Cullum).

A native of Jackson, Mississippi, Geary is the youngest of four children in what she describes as an "All-American family." Encouraged at an early age by her mother, a voice and music teacher, Geary studied ballet, voice and piano while starring in all of her school's musical productions since the age of six.

Geary earned a Bachelor of Arts degree in vocal performance and graduated with honors from the University of Mississippi. While attending summer school at UCLA during her sophomore year of college, Geary fell in love with the West Coast. After relocating to Los Angeles upon graduation, she waited tables while honing her craft. In classic Hollywood fashion, she was discovered by a talent manager who helped launch her professional career.

Her acting career began with a series of national commercials including Coke and General Motors. After landing the lead role in *Senior Prom,* a two-person play at the Off-Ramp Theatre in Los Angeles, Geary moved on to television where she guest starred on the popular daytime soap, *The Young and the Restless, Divorce Court, Adam 12,* and *Superior Court,* among others.

Geary's feature film credits include *Rich Girl, Dangerous Curves, War Dancing,* and *For the Love of Mike.* Geary currently resides near Seattle, Washington, and enjoys singing and working out in her spare time.

Elaine Miles

Elaine Miles portrays Marilyn Whirlwind, Dr. Joel Fleischman's (Rob Morrow) quietly sage assistant. Marilyn's subtle persistence and calm demeanor is the perfect foil to Fleischman's neurotic behavior. From the moment they meet at Cicely's makeshift medical office where Marilyn insists on applying for and accepting a job which Fleischman claims doesn't exist, the doctor knows he has met his match.

Born on April 7 in Pendleton, Oregon, Miles was raised outside the Seattle area as a member of the Umatilla tribe, one of three tribes on her reservation. Brought up traditionally with her parents' Indian heritage, one-half Cayuse and one-half Nez Perce, Miles learned her Native American culture through ancestral storytelling.

Skilled in the traditional activities of her tribe, beading, pottery and weaving, Miles is also a prize-winning traditional dancer, placing second in Women's International Buckskin dancing in the Goodwill Games held in Everett, Washington.

With no previous acting experience, Miles was discovered by *Northern Exposure*'s casting agents when she accompanied her mother Armenia Miles and other local Native Americans who were auditioning for the part of Marilyn. After seeing her in the waiting room, the agents asked her to read for the part. They immediately gave her the role of Marilyn, while they cast her mother in the recurring role of Mrs. Anku, Ed's (Darren E. Burrows) aunt and wife of the local medicine man. ·

Darren E. Burrows

Darren E. Burrows portrays Ed Chigliak, a young Native American who helps Dr. Joel Fleischman (Rob Morrow) adjust to his new rural environment. Possessing an uncanny sense of timing, Ed often appears out of nowhere, spouting bits of wisdom gleaned from the many films he has watched. His unclouded, naive observations and 180 I.Q. lend a colorful contrast to Dr. Fleischman's inbred obstinance.

Like his character, Burrows is of Native American heritage. Born on September 12 in Winfield, Kansas, Burrows is one-quarter Cherokee and one-quarter Apache Indian. After experiencing the simple pleasures of small town life in Kansas, Burrows was eager to "see the world," prompting him to head west to California.

After spending a few years exploring various avenues of employment, Burrows decided to try his luck in the acting profession. Soon after joining the Billy Drago/Silvana Gallardo Acting workshop, he landed his first professional acting job in the horror film *976-EVIL*.

For his next role he spent three months in Thailand filming Brian De Palma's *Casualties of War* with Michael J. Fox and Sean Penn, in which he played Cherry, a naive member of the combat platoon. His additional film credits include starring roles in *Class of 1999* and John Waters's *Cry Baby* with Johnny Depp for Imagine Entertainment.

Burrows' television credits include a recurring role on the CBS series *TV 101*, and guest starring roles on *Hard Times on Planet Earth* and *Dragnet*.

He has also performed in the Los Angeles stage productions of *Dark of the Moon* at the Crown Upton Dinner Theater and in *Simpson Street* at the Los Angeles Workshop.

Darren currently resides in Bellevue, Washington, and is an avid outdoorsman. In his free time he enjoys camping and motorcycle and horseback riding. He is a fan of Western rodeos and has recently begun to learn roping techniques.

Peg Phillips

Peg Phillips portrays Ruth-Anne Miller, a wise seventy-five-year-old storekeeper who dispenses psychological insight with each purchase. A woman who has lived through it all and has learned to appreciate life for everything it has to offer, Ruth-Anne provides a constant in an always turbulent town. Proprietor of a one-stop shop which serves as everything from the library, post office, and local market, to the video store, Ruth-Anne with her quiet strength, wise words, and life experiences guides the town through their many crazy predicaments.

A native of Everett, Washington, Phillips left the state of Washington at the age of twenty and in the next twenty years married, divorced, raised four children by herself and helped raise her four grandchildren. Knowing from the age of four that she always wanted to act, she participated in a few community theater productions. But not until her family was grown did she return to the Seattle area and have the opportunity to live her dream. At the age of sixty-five, Phillips enrolled in the University of Washington Drama School and hired an agent. Her immediate success did not allow her to finish her degree, although she plans to complete it by the time she turns eighty.

Her numerous film credits include: *Waiting for the Light* starring Shirley MacLaine, *Plainclothes* with Abe Vigoda, *Dangerous Affections* with Judith Light, and *Chase* with Jennifer O'Neill. Her theater credits include *Romeo and Juliet*, performed at the Marin Shakespeare Festival; *Night Mother* at the University of Washington, and *Madwoman of Chaillot* at the Santa Cruz Repertory.

Throughout her long life, Phillips has lived everywhere from New York to Honolulu to California, but in her heart she knew she would return to Washington. At the moment she is living her dream—working as a very successful actress on a highly-acclaimed, Emmy Award-winning television series which almost films in her own backyard.

In her spare time and during her breaks from the show, she enjoys two very special pastimes: "gardening and grandchildren!"

THE EPISODES

Northern Exposure's first "season," in July and August of 1990, was just eight episodes long. Its second, in April and May of 1991, nearly a year later, was only seven.

Then, the series caught on, moving from cult hit to ratings winner, and it was back on that fall, with a twenty-three-episode order for the 1991–92 season.

Before premiere week of the 1992–93 season, CBS, recognizing the show's value as the capstone of its vaunted Monday night prime-time schedule, gave its producers TV-land's highest accolade: a rare, *fifty*-episode, two-season order. As the season got underway, it won the Emmy as Best Drama Series.

What follows are the *Northern Exposure* episode synopses (through December 1992), normally seen only by industry insiders. Incidentally, a "log line" is the one-sentence episode summary you might find in a television guide.

SEASON ONE
(7/12/90–8/30/90)

PILOT

Log Line:

Dr. Joel Flesichman, an inveterate New Yorker, arrives in Alaska with plans to fulfill his medical school financing obligation by practicing in metropolitan Anchorage. However, he is quickly informed that his services are not needed in Anchorage, but in a small, remote village by the name of Cicely.

Synopsis:

As soon as Dr. Fleischman (Rob Morrow) sets his eyes upon the small town of Cicely, Alaska, his "fish out of water" experience begins. From the ride into town with Ed Chigliak (Darren E. Burrows), a backwoods yet worldly Native American who professes an affinity for rhythm and blues, to the oil and water relationship he develops immediately with his attractive landlady, local bush pilot Maggie O'Connell (Janine Turner), Fleischman encounters more than he can handle, despite his urban roots. When he tries to finagle a way out of his contract through legal loopholes, he is quickly and definitively informed by a gun-wielding town patriarch, retired astronaut Maurice Minnifield (Barry Corbin), that leaving is not an option.

Written by Josh Brand and John Falsey
Directed by Josh Brand
Airdate: July 12, 1990

"BRAINS, KNOW-HOW AND NATIVE INTELLIGENCE"

Log Line:

While Joel is struggling with evergrowing frustration over faulty plumbing in his cabin, he sensitively deals with Ed's uncle Anku, a proud but ill medicine man who is reluctant to embrace modern medicine.

Synopsis:

Joel's futile effort to handle his cabin's plumbing problems on his own provide a great source of amusement for Maggie. Meanwhile, at Ed's request, Joel attempts to treat his Uncle Anku's (guest star Frank Sotonoma Salsedo) deteriorating health with little success. Averse to modern medicine, the Indian elder tests Joel's schooled, medical expertise.

At KBHR, the storefront radio station, anger and unrest develops among the townsfolk when Maurice fires deejay Chris-in-the-morning (John Corbett) and takes over the station controls himself—playing nonstop show tunes.

Written by Stuart Stevens
Directed by Peter O'Fallon
Airdate: July 19, 1990

"SOAPY SANDERSON"

Log Line:

After the passing of one of Cicely's most-loved eccentrics, Soapy Sanderson, Joel and Maggie battle over the proper handling of his one hundred acres of land, left to them in his will.

Synopsis:

When Soapy Sanderson (guest star John McLiam), one of the town's most-loved eccentrics, dies, he leaves his land and prized huskies to both Joel and Maggie. At first, Maggie is impressed at Joel's noble gesture to give the land back to the Native Americans. So impressed, that she actually warms up to Joel over an expensive bottle of wine. But the flame is put out quickly when she discovers that Joel has arranged to sell the land for $50,000 to business-minded Indian Chief Ronkonkoma (guest star Julian Fox), who intends to use the land as a tax write-off.

Much to Ed's delight, two student filmmakers (guest stars Darryl Fong and Christina Miller) from Kenyon College arrive to document the life of Soapy, who earned two doctorate degrees from the college and was a major benefactor.

Written by Karen Hall, from a story by
Karen Hall and Jerry Stahl
Directed by Steve Cragg
Airdate: July 26, 1990

"DREAMS, SCHEMES AND PUTTING GREENS"

Log Line:

Holling gets cold feet and leaves a pregnant Shelly at the altar, while Joel and Maurice try to make a deal with visiting Japanese businessmen to build a resort in Cicely.

Synopsis:

Bar owner Holling Vincoeur (John Cullum) proposes to Shelly Tambo (Cynthia Geary) after learning that she is carrying his child. But he gets cold feet just before the ceremony and leaves the bride, Shelly; maid of honor, Maggie; best man, Joel; and a church full of people in shock.

Meanwhile, Joel joins Maurice in wooing a group of Japanese businessmen to build a golf resort in Cicely, after striking a deal with Maurice to include him in as a well-paid "attending physician" at the resort.

Written by Sean Clark
Directed by Dan Lerner
Airdate: August 2, 1990

"THE RUSSIAN FLU"

Log Line:

A flu epidemic sweeps through Cicely and threatens to ruin Joel's romantic weekend with his visiting fiancée, Elaine.

Synopsis:

While Fleischman works to help the ailing citizens of Cicely, he tries desperately to find time for a romantic interlude with Elaine (guest star Jessica Lundy), his visiting fiancée. Meanwhile, Maggie befriends Elaine and keeps her occupied while Joel unsuccessfully tries to stop the mysterious flu from spreading.

Thankfully, Marilyn Whirlwind (Elaine Miles), Fleischman's very practical nurse, finally takes control and dispenses an old Indian folk remedy that manages to do what modern medicine couldn't. A skeptical Joel is only convinced of the remedy's merit when it cures Elaine's flu, just in time for her return to New York.

Written by David Assael
Directed by David Carson
Airdate: August 9, 1990

"SEX, LIES AND ED'S TAPES"

Log Line:

Holling and Shelly are caught off guard when Shelly's husband Wayne, a nineteen-year-old hockey player, arrives in town asking for a divorce. Meanwhile, Ed struggles to write a Hollywood blockbuster movie.

Synopsis:

Holling is shocked to learn that Shelly is a married woman. When her young husband, Wayne (guest star Brandon Douglas), shows up asking for a divorce, Shelly tells Holling that it's not a big deal. She just forgot to let him know about the marriage. An honorable man, Holling tells a confused Shelly that they cannot cohabitate until her divorce is final, clearing the way for Wayne to woo Shelly once again.

Meanwhile, Ed struggles with screenwriter's block while trying to create Hollywood's next big hit.

Written by Josh Brand and John Falsey
Directed by Sandy Smolan
Airdate: August 16, 1990

"A KODIAK MOMENT"

Log Line:

While Maurice ponders life and death after his only brother passes away, Joel and Maggie administer childbirth classes to a group of native Alaskans in a neighboring remote village. Meanwhile, Holling finds out that "Jesse the Bear" has been sighted and vows to take care of him, once and for all.

Synopsis:

Feeling a great sense of loss after the death of his brother and only kin, Malcolm, Maurice decides to appoint a new beneficiary to the Minnifield fortune. After giving orphaned Chris a try as his heir, Maurice decides that he is not up to Minnifield standards and vows to live forever, instead. At the same time, Joel and Maggie experience the miracle of birth together in a neighboring remote village. Meanwhile, Ed helps Holling and loyal companion Shelly track the famed "Jesse the Bear."

Written by Steve Wasserman and Jessica Klein
Directed by Max Tash
Airdate: August 23, 1990

"THE AURORA BOREALIS"

Log Line:

Joel learns of the legend of "Adam," a Bigfoot-like creature who walks the woods outside of Cicely. Meanwhile, Chris bonds with a black traveler passing through town, who turns out to be the brother he never knew he had, literally.

Synopsis:

Joel comes face-to-face with the legendary "Adam" (guest star Adam Arkin), a Bigfoot-like character whose mythical existence has haunted Cicely for years. When Joel claims to have been rescued by the giant, whom he describes as a real person and a damn good cook, his sanity is seriously questioned by the townspeople.

Meanwhile, a black stranger named Bernard (guest star Richard Cummings, Jr.) rides into town on a motorcycle and immediately connects with Chris, helping him to build an elaborate metal sculpture in honor of the Aurora Borealis (Northern Lights), due to appear soon. After spending much time together, the two artists discover, through a bizarre twist of fate, that they have the same biological father.

Written by Charles Rosin
Directed by Peter O'Fallon
Airdate: August 30, 1990

"GOODBYE TO ALL THAT"

Log Line:

Joel receives a "Dear John" letter from his fiancée Elaine, while Holling's gift to Shelly—a satellite dish—turns her into a TV addict.

Synopsis:

When Joel receives a "Dear John" letter from Elaine, he slowly begins to fall apart. Attempting to hide his misery from the all- knowing townspeople, he looks to Chris for help in "jumping back into the pond." But after a double date with two Ivy League coeds fails, Joel commits himself to bed and wallows in his misery. A worried Ed visits Joel and listens to him reminisce about his relationship with Elaine. When Joel reveals that he can't get over his heartbreak unless he has some kind of closure, Ed vows to help, once Joel explains what closure is.

Ed convinces Holling and Maggie to help him recreate a scenario at Joel and Elaine's favorite sidewalk cafe, with Maggie acting as Elaine, to give Joel the opportunity to say all the things he wanted to say to her.

Meanwhile, Holling buys a satellite dish for Shelly who "wants to see the world" and unknowingly creates a monster. Watching every obscure channel she can find, Shelly neglects Holling, her job, and sleep while she remains hypnotized in front of the TV screen. Finally, she confesses her obsession to Chris, the closest thing Cicely has to a priest, and seeks forgiveness.

Written by Robin Green
Directed by Stuart Margolin
Airdate: April 8, 1991

"THE BIG KISS"

Log Line:

A wise Indian spirit helps Ed in his search to find his parents, while Chris loses his voice to a mysterious beautiful woman.

Synopsis:

"One Who Waits" (guest star Floyd Red Crow Westerman), a wise old spirit seen only by the Indians, accompanies Ed through town as they search for the identities of Ed's natural parents. Meanwhile, Chris loses his voice at the sight of a beautiful stranger and Cicely loses its favorite deejay. When "One Who Waits" offers an old Indian remedy for regaining his voice—sleep with the most beautiful girl in town—Chris is taken aback. But, desperate to speak again, he agrees to follow the logic—if beauty took his voice away, then beauty will restore it.

However, when he sheepishly turns to Maggie for help, the whole town sits up and takes notice. Especially Fleischman, who exacerbates the situation by doubting Maggie's ability to help Chris regain his voice.

Written by Henry Bromell
Directed by Sandy Smolan
Airdate: April 15, 1991

"ALL IS VANITY"

Log Line:

Maggie tries to win her father's approval by pretending that Joel, a successful doctor, is her boyfriend. Meanwhile, Holling contemplates circumcision to please Shelly.

Synopsis:

When Maggie discovers that her father is coming for a visit, she panics. In an attempt to gain his approval, Maggie has been sending letters home describing Joel, a successful doctor, as her boyfriend. Although she convinces Joel to play along, she hates the fact that he has glimpsed this part of her personal life, especially when Joel seems to enjoy the charade. Finally, it becomes too much to deal with and Maggie tells her father the truth: that her boyfriend is Rick, an uneducated bush pilot.

Meanwhile, Holling struggles with the decision to have a circumcision when Shelly comments that she has never known a man who hasn't had it done.

Written by Andrew Schneider and Diane Frolov
Directed by Nick Marck
Airdate: April 22, 1991

"WHAT I DID FOR LOVE"

Log Line:

Maggie dreams of Joel's death in a plane crash as he prepares for a trip back to his native New York. Maurice continues a long-time affair with an astronaut groupie.

Synopsis:

Joel thinks twice about a scheduled visit to New York when the townspeople take exceptionally well to his substitute, a Jewish doctor from New York. However, the similarities between the two end there. Dr. Gingsberg (guest star Leo Geter), a strapping blond man with an engaging smile, charms the residents of Cicely immediately, leaving Joel feeling jealous.

Maggie, meanwhile, is reluctant to warn Joel of the dreams she has been having of his impending death in a plane crash. But feeling compelled, she warns him not to fly anywhere. As she expected and dreaded, Joel interprets it to mean that Maggie has feelings for him.

Maurice tries to keep his ongoing affair with a married astronaut groupie (guest star Elizabeth Huddle) a secret from the town.

Written by Ellen Herman
Directed by Steve Robman
Airdate: April 29, 1991

"SPRING BREAK"

Log Line:

Temporary madness sweeps through Cicely as the townfolk await the ice meltdown and the arrival of spring.

Synopsis:

The citizens of Cicely are overcome with fits of inexplicable craziness as they anxiously await for the arrival of spring, marked by the breaking of the ice. The first sign of madness is the return of a mysterious kleptomaniac who strikes only during the meltdown each year. While Ed plays amateur detective and tries to track down the thief, the rest of the townfolk are seemingly out of control.

Maurice falls for Sergeant Semanski (guest star Diane Delano), a female state trooper sent to investigate the town's thefts, who is more of a man than Maurice is. Holling tries feverishly to instigate fights with just about everybody, while Shelly uncharacteristically dives into classic literature. Maggie tries to ignore her numerous sexual fantasies of Joel by fervently knitting and cooking, while Joel—whose libido is on overdrive—becomes obsessed with satisfying his carnal desires. The extended period of madness culminates with the annual "Running of the Bulls," when the men of Cicely run through town in freezing temperature stark naked.

Written by David Assael
Directed by Rob Thompson
Airdate: May 6, 1991

"WAR AND PEACE"

Log Line:

Passages from *War and Peace* are woven into the lives of Cicely's residents and visitors, who experience Tolstoyesque nightmares and Dostoyevskian passions.

Synopsis:

When old friend, Nikolai Ivanovich Appollanov (guest star Elya Baskin), comes to town for his yearly visit, Cicely's townfolk are thrilled, all except Maurice Minnifield. While the rest of Cicely is embracing the arrival of their musically gifted friend and his Slavic influence with gusto, Maurice's hell-bent patriotism leads him to challenge the town's adopted Russkie to a duel.

While Holling struggles to overcome his dream-riddled nights by following Tolstoy's example and doing something reckless and wild, Ed experiences something reckless and wild of his own—first love. Smitten by a red-haired preacher's daughter named Lightfeather (guest star Dana Andersen), Ed woos her with love letters penned by his prolific friend, deejay Chris Stevens.

Written by Robin Green and Henry Bromell
Directed by Bill D'Elia
Airdate: May 13, 1991

"SLOW DANCE"

Log Line:

The curse of Maggie has struck again and poor Rick is the victim of "death by falling satellite."

Synopsis:

While the townpeople mourn the tragic, yet strangely humorous, death of Rick (guest star Grant Goodeve), they avoid Maggie like the plague. It takes a bold, not altogether willing, move by Fleischman to dispel the fear that Maggie is a cursed woman.

Meanwhile, two men (guest stars Don McManus and Doug Ballard) looking to buy a house in Cicely discover they have a lot more in common with Maurice than he would like to admit, including a love of show tunes and gourmet cooking.

In the meantime, Shelly feels like a third wheel when Holling reminisces with an old gal from his hometown.

Written by Diane Frolov and Andrew Schneider
Directed by David Carson
Airdate: May 20, 1991

"THE BUMPY ROAD TO LOVE"

Log Line:

Maggie discovers the late Rick was unfaithful and proceeds to distrust all men; Maurice's tax indiscretion could destroy his relationship with Officer Semanski; while Joel is toted off to the woods to play marriage counselor to wildman-chef extraordinaire Adam and his hypochrondiacal wife, Eve.

Synopsis:

At the unveiling of Rick's memorial statue, Maggie meets a woman she never knew existed—Rick's other lover. Maggie goes on an anti-men campaign, and gets herself incredibly drunk. Ruth-Anne (Peg Phillips) nurses her back from her hangover and teaches her a valuable lesson about men. Maggie eventually comes to terms with Rick's infidelity and suddenly the angst-ridden Joel starts to look much better.

Adam pays a midnight call on Joel, insisting Fleischman return with him to his cabin to examine his wife Eve (guest star Valerie Mahaffey), a hypochondriac of epic proportions. Irate with his wife's litany of pseudo-symptoms, Adam storms off, leaving Joel behind in the cabin. But Eve has other plans for the good doctor—she intends to keep Joel shackled to the cabin wall so she can have a twenty-four-hour on-call physician. Adam returns, but only to collect his things. Suddenly, Joel is forced to become a marriage mediator, as his only way of escape is to get this odd couple back together.

Maurice gives state trooper Barbara Semanski engraved twin Browning handguns as a token of his undying love. But when she discovers that Maurice may have cheated on his income tax, Semanski, a staunch protector of justice, refuses to have anything to do with him.

Written by Martin Sage and Sybil Adelman
Directed by Nick Marck
Airdate: September 23, 1991

"ONLY YOU"

Log Line:

Chris emits a sexual scent which causes all women to lust after him—all but the visiting optometrist. Perplexed by her lack of attraction, Chris suddenly wants only her. Maurice once again accuses Holling of stealing Shelly from him, leaving only Shelly to set the record straight.

Synopsis:

Chris goes into "heat," emitting a seductive scent which attracts women of all types from near and far. A periodic affliction of Stevens men, Chris is prepared for the onslaught of women mesmerized by his smell. Joel is also fascinated by this biological phenomenon and launches into a scent study of his own. But just as Chris is beginning to enjoy it all, he meets visiting optometrist Dr. Irene Rondenet (guest star Caitlin Clarke), who is unfazed by his sexual scent. Perplexed by her lack of attraction, Chris stops enjoying the women who want him because he wants the one who doesn't.

Holling takes a photo of Maurice which is to be hung in the portrait gallery of the NASA Space Center. Maurice hates the photo and accuses Holling of purposefully taking an ugly picture of him. He also dredges up the fact that Holling took Shelly from him. Both men have their own version of what happened when Maurice brought Shelly to Cicely, but it takes Shelly, with her own version, to set them both straight.

Maggie has her own problems when Dr. Rondenet diagnoses her as farsighted and in need of reading glasses. Suddenly Maggie feels she's over-the-hill.

Written by Ellen Herman
Directed by Bill D'Elia
Airdate: September 30, 1991

"OY WILDERNESS"

Log Line:

Joel is a reluctant survival student when he and Maggie become stranded in the wilderness. Shelly's best friend Cyndy comes to Cicely asking Shelly to divorce Wayne, because Cyndy has been married to him for six months.

Synopsis:

While Joel and Maggie are flying back from an Eskimo vaccination trip, her plane's engine fails and they are forced to make an emergency landing somewhere in the Alaskan wilderness. Joel is definitely at odds with nature so Maggie tries teaching him some basic survival skills—like what not to eat or touch—but Joel is too busy worrying about being attacked by anything furry. As the

days pass, he submits to eating squirrel roasted over an open campfire and further surprises Maggie when he uses his surgical technique to get her plane engine going again.

Cyndy Rincon (guest star Christine Elise), Shelly's best friend, arrives in Cicely announcing that she and Wayne have been married for six months and only recently did Cyndy find out Shelly never divorced him. But Shelly resolutely refuses to divorce Wayne. Shelly, always the most popular girl, finds it difficult to accept that Cyndy has taken her place and is living the life she used to—while she is residing in Cicely. Cyndy explains how difficult it was to always be second best while Shelly reveals it wasn't great being perfect either. Realizing life goes on, Shelly agrees to divorce Wayne and asks Chris to perform the unknotting—since he has the power to join people in marriage, he should also have the power to tear it asunder.

Written by Robin Green
Directed by Miles Watkins
Airdate: October 7, 1991

"ANIMALS R US"

Log Line:

Maggie is confronted with the strange possibility that the late Rick has been reincarnated as a dog; Maurice sees big profits in big eggs when he discovers Marilyn owns an ostrich herd; and Ed seriously considers getting out of show business.

Synopsis:

A big, beautiful, blue-eyed malamute comes to visit Maggie and won't leave her alone. Maggie is charmed by the canine and feels rather strange because it's as if she's known this dog for years. When it hops up on Rick's stool at Holling's Bar and eats beef jerky just like Rick did, Maggie begins to notice similarities between the dog's behavior and Rick's, but immediately dismisses the notion of reincarnation. After a series of strange coincidences, Maggie asks the dog if he is Rick, to which he barks his affirmation. Suddenly Maggie is confronted with the possibility that her dead lover has been reincarnated as a stray dog—something everyone, except Fleischman, is willing to accept.

Maurice discovers that Marilyn owns a herd of ostriches which lay eggs the size of basketballs and proposes a business partnership. But Maurice's big business idea cracks when Marilyn finds out that the ostriches dislike him.

Despite encouragement from the locals as well as his pen pals Woody Allen, Steven Spielberg, and Martin Scorsese, Ed almost pulls the plug on his film but decides to screen it for the town instead.

Written by Robin Green
Directed by Nick Marck
Airdate: October 14, 1991

"JULES ET JOEL"

Log Line:

Joel's twin brother, Jules, a charming but conniving rogue, creates a stir when he arrives in quiet Cicely to visit his sibling.

Synopsis:

Joel's (Rob Morrow) twin brother, Jules (also Rob Morrow), his complete antithesis, arrives in town for a brief vacation from himself, literally. After Jules convinces a reluctant Joel that it will be harmless, the two brothers switch identities and proceed to fool everyone in town. While the new "Joel" hits on Maggie, the new "Jules" indulges in his repressed wild side and pays the price, in jail.

Meanwhile, Chris's new "Mea Culpa" call-in radio show goes a little too far when a crazed caller (guest star Raymond O'Connor) confesses to a string of bombings and wants to turn himself in, but only to Chris.

Written by Stuart Stevens
Directed by Jim Hayman
Airdate: October 28, 1991

"THE BODY IN QUESTION"

Log Line:

A frozen body discovered in the local river could cause a world-wide historical revolution: was Napoleon Bonaparte at Waterloo or was he ice fishing near Cicely and fathering a tribe of French-speaking Native Americans?

Synopsis:

Chris discovers the body of a man dressed in eighteenth century costume frozen in a block of ice. Maurice keeps this "find" frozen at Hollings Bar until they figure out what to do with him. Holling and Maggie translate the man's journal, written in French, which says that "Pierre" and his close friend Napoleon Bonaparte were in Alaska fishing during the Battle of Waterloo. To confuse history even more, the diary says that the Little Emperor fathered a child with an Indian woman. Marilyn confirms there is a local tribe of French-speaking Indians called the Tellakutans. The Tellakutans later arrive to claim the body of their folkloric hero, but Maurice will not give it up without a fight—he has visions of tourists swarming all over Cicely to see the entombed body of the man who has rewritten history.

All this talk of royalty has caused Holling to become aloof to Shelly because he is afraid to tell her he is descended from a line of dastardly noblemen. Meanwhile, Shelly fears Holling is shying away because she may be infertile. Joel is also touched by the historical discussion as he realizes he is the embodiment of his ancestors' struggles and triumphs.

While doing stock work for Ruth-Anne, Ed tells her he is questioning his talent because of the opinions of others. Ruth-Anne tells him to follow his heart, knowing from experience what happens when you don't.

Written by Henry Bromell
Directed by David Carson
Airdate: November 4, 1991

"ROOTS"

Log Line:

Joel grapples with the possibility of a new start with his old love when his ex-fiancée Elaine visits Cicely; Bernard brings Chris his inheritance from their father, giving Chris the opportunity to go to Africa, as his dreams have told him to; and Adam becomes the chef at Holling's Bar.

Synopsis:

Joel's ex-fiancée Elaine comes to Cicely after the death of her husband with hopes of sorting out the mess she made out of their breakup. Bitter and resentful, Joel is at first unwilling to forgive her. But Elaine has been an integral part of his life since the third grade and slowly he realizes it is not over between them. He begins to feel like old times. Suddenly Joel and Elaine are faced with the sobering possibility of starting over.

Bernard returns to visit Chris and give him his half of his father's inheritance. Chris has been having strange, vivid dreams of African dancers and concludes that the money can now make the dream a reality. But as Chris is making travel reservations, he realizes his psychic wires have once again crossed with his half-brother's and Africa is Bernard's destiny, not his.

Adam hits Joel up for $100 to pay an insurance premium. But when Joel refuses, Adam resorts to desperate measures—he bets Holling $100 that he could have people lining up around the restaurant to get in. The diners of Cicely are in for a culinary treat.

Written by Dennis Koenig and Jordan Budde
Directed by Sandy Smolan
Airdate: November 11, 1991

"A-HUNTING WE WILL GO"

Log Line:

After grousing about the hunting frenzy sweeping Cicely, Joel sees firsthand what it's all about by outfitting himself to join Chris and Holling for the primal ritual in the wilds. Holling, however, prefers the home fires to the campfire, while, back in town, Ed fears that Ruth-Anne is being stalked by the Grim Reaper.

Synopsis:

Joel Fleischman is repulsed when he sees Maggie driving into town with a large deer she shot strapped across the hood of her truck. He continues his debate about the evils of hunting with Holling and Chris, who maintains that being a hunter is man's natural place in the food chain. In order to form a fair and scientific conclusion, Joel decides to join Chris and Holling on their upcoming hunt.

So Joel and Chris, armed with rifles, and Holling, with his camera, head off into the woods, seeking grouse. Chris flushes out a flock and kills two. Joel misses. Holling and Chris are satisfied, but Joel wants the entire primal experience and, suddenly, turns into the Terminator, wanting to kill anything that moves. When he gets his big chance, he only wings a bird. He then tries to save its life, but the bird dies of shock. Reluctantly, Joel admits to Maggie that the hunting was great—it was the killing he couldn't accept.

When Ed Chigliak finds out that Ruth-Anne has just turned seventy-five, he begins to treat her like a frail old woman. Struck by mortality, Ed decides to give her a present that will last forever.

Written by Craig Volk
Directed by Bill D'Elia
Airdate: November 18, 1991

"GET REAL"

Log Line:

Magic is in the air when the circus comes to Cicely. Marilyn becomes romantically involved with The Flying Man, while Holling fears his passion for Shelly may be waning when he realizes her feet are big.

Synopsis:

The circus comes to Cicely when the bus carrying the "Ludgwig Wittgenstein Masquerade and Reality Company" breaks down. The Flying Man Enrico Bellati (guest star Bill Irwin) takes a shine to Marilyn, but she refuses to go out with him. The mute Bellati is persistent and Marilyn eventually agrees to have dinner with him at her parents' house. Marilyn's parents like him, and Marilyn admits she does, too. But when Bellati asks her to join him on the road, Marilyn is torn between staying in Cicely or seeing the world with The Flying Man.

When Joel's medical school alumni newsletter arrives filled with the exploits of underachievers who now have posh Park Avenue jobs, he starts feeling like a prisoner of Alaska. So to make the most of his time in the wilderness, Joel begins an intensive study program to specialize in endocrinology. Now when he returns to New York, everyone who's anyone will know Dr. Joel Fleischman.

For the first time, Holling notices Shelly's feet are big—a sign that his passion for Shelly may be waning. So he asks her to marry him in an attempt to salve his conscience. Shelly sees through his ploy, but is hurt when he tells her he did it because her feet aren't attractive any longer. Shelly seeks comfort from Maggie who gives her a less than optimistic pep talk on the joys of singlehood, leaving Shelly to rethink her options.

Written by Diane Frolov and Andrew Schneider
Directed by Michael Katleman
Airdate: December 9, 1991

"SEOUL MATES"

Log Line:

Maurice, dreading being alone for the holidays, gets a big surprise when his gift is an instant family of his own. Meanwhile Maggie, dreading being with her family, gets a big surprise when her parents opt for a Caribbean Christmas without her.

Synopsis:

Maurice gets a Holiday surprise when a Korean family arrives in Cicely. Bon Joo (guest star Chi-Muoi Lo) tells Maurice his father, Duk Won (guest star James Song), is Maurice's son and his grandmother, Yong Ja (guest star Kim Kim), is Maurice's former lover. When the paternity tests check out, Maurice is deeply disturbed. He has always dreamed of a son to carry on the Minnifield name, but now that he has one, Maurice is unsure he wants him—mainly because he's not white. Just as the family is about to leave, Maurice decides to make a real effort to get to know

his son—despite the communication barrier. Suddenly, Maurice begins to realize the greatness of the gift he has received.

Maggie dreads going home for Christmas where she will hear over and over who got married to who and who has a new baby. But when she picks up her parents' letter, expecting a round trip ticket to Michigan, she learns they are going to St. Thomas, leaving her to face the holidays alone. Maggie claims she's relieved she won't have to face the trials of family when she's really crushed that her parents cancelled Christmas.

As a child Joel longed for a Christmas tree, but his traditional Jewish parents would never allow it. So this year, Joel decides to put a tree in his living room. However, once the tree arrives, he doesn't know what to do with it. Despite his affection for the symbol, Joel feels it just doesn't belong to him, so he takes the tree fully decorated to Maggie's house as a surprise.

Shelly misses her Roman Catholic roots and longs for a High Christmas mass. So Holling fills Cicely's Unitarian church with Catholic icons and sings a Latin mass for Shelly himself.

Written by Diane Frolov and Andrew Schneider
Directed by Jack Bender
Airdate: December 16, 1991

"DATELINE: CICELY"

Log Line:

Maurice goes out on a limb to spice up his newspaper's coverage by hiring an unnamed reporter given to clandestine meetings. Maggie talks to trees, but Joel won't listen, and to ease Holling's tax debts, Chris become a partner at the Brick, where he sets about sprucing up the place.

Synopsis:

Maurice starts a local campaign to support the *Cicely News and World Telegram*. To spark public interest in the paper, he hires Adam as his anonymous writer. Adam's first story is about talking trees, which causes the paper's sales to go sky high. A follow-up story on botanical espionage by the government brings a defamation lawsuit by the Justice Department, as well as a 400 percent increase in sales. In addition, a Japanese multinational corporation buys six months of advertising in advance. But just when the paper is expanding into two sections, ace reporter Adam disappears, sending circulation into a tailspin.

Holling is in trouble with the IRS for not paying taxes since 1959. Willing to own up to his debt to the government, but somewhat short on cash, he asks Chris to buy half-interest in the bar. Chris, who has been feeling a bit down lately, gratefully jumps at the chance to become a tavern half-owner. However, he goes overboard with his new ideas to enhance business, and suddenly Holling feels out of place in his own bar. But before being asked by Holling to stop what he is doing, Chris confesses that he wants out of the bar business because it simply does not feel right.

Written by Jeff Melvoin
Directed by Michael Fresco
Airdate: January 6, 1992

"OUR TRIBE"

Log Line:

Joel reluctantly undergoes a cultural conversion after receiving a goat as a gift from a grateful village elder, who insists on "adopting" him into her tribe, and a mysterious Holling shuts down the Brick, ostensibly to wax the floors.

Synopsis:

When Joel gracefully tries to refuse a goat as payment for treatment, Mrs. Noanuk (guest star Rosetta Pintado), the tribal elder, opts for a bigger reward—making Joel a member of her tribe! Joel still doesn't want to become an Indian, and Mrs. Noanuk takes this as an insult to her tribe and ancestors. Marilyn also takes this as an affront and gives Joel the silent treatment until he finally relents. The first thing he has to do is give away all his worldly possessions. Thinking it is only a symbolic giving away, Joel allows many of his belongings to be taken away and later becomes very upset when some of his things show up at a garage sale. Next, he must fast, then he has to go into the woods at night, with Ed as his guide, to search for his vision—only then can he be initiated into the tribe as Heals With Tools.

Meanwhile, Holling sends Shelly to Saskatoon, claiming he needs to refinish the floor, and closes up the bar. Maggie becomes suspicious when Holling starts receiving secret packages. She sneaks in one night and discovers that Holling is searching the night sky with a telescope. He tells her he is looking for a star he bought for Eleanor almost forty years ago. She was the most remarkable woman he ever knew, and he tried to let her know where to look in the sky. Eventually, a friend wrote that Eleanor had died. This is the last chance he has to see the star before it fades into astral oblivion. He intended to keep this a secret from everyone and asks Maggie to keep the secret with him.

Written by David Assael
Directed by Lee Shallet
Airdate: January 13, 1992

"THINGS BECOME EXTINCT"

Log Line:

A study in self-examination brings on a mid-life crisis for Holling, opens up another door for Ed, and leaves Joel feeling culturally isolated.

Synopsis:

Ed answers an ad in the *Filmmakers* magazine to film a vanishing breed—or something that is vanishing. He will receive film credit and $50. Now the problem is to find something that is about to become extinct! Finally, he meets Ira Wingfeather (guest star Bryson Liberty) who carves wooden flutes—a dying art. While Ed films Wingfeather's work, he becomes intrigued by the craftsmanship and the history associated with making the flutes. Wingfeather tells him he is the last of the line. His children have no desire to carry on the craft because they have a different life and different music. Wingfeather accepts this as part of life and the cycle of creation and extinction. Ed, however, is troubled at the thought of such beauty being extinguished forever and realizes it is up to him to save it.

While trying to prove to Ed that Jews are not a vanishing Alaskan breed, Joel discovers the scarcity of Jewish names in the local telephone books. He finds there are only two thousand Jews in the entire state of Alaska. But Joel's newfound obsession with finding Alaskan Jews causes him to feel even more isolated than before. Meanwhile, Holling becomes depressed when he gets the news that his Uncle Charlie died—a man who boldly lived his life. Pondering his own mortality, Holling feels life has passed him by and regrets he did not live it as fully as his uncle did. With the help of some 100-proof homemade vodka, Holling takes to the hills where he wallows in a deep mid-life crisis.

Written by Robin Green, from a story
by Mitchell Burgess
Directed by Dean Parisot
Airdate: January 20, 1992

"BURNING DOWN THE HOUSE"

Log Line:

Maggie receives a double dose of disaster when her mother accidentally burns down her house after announcing she is divorcing Maggie's father. Meanwhile, Chris searches for the "right" cow as part of his new piece of performance art.

Synopsis:

Maggie's mother (guest star Bibi Besch) comes for a visit and announces that she and Maggie's father are divorcing after thirty-two years of marriage. Maggie is upset at the news and rushes out of her house, leaving her mother behind. However, while she is in town, her mother manages to set Maggie's house on fire, razing the structure and burning all of Maggie's possessions: her clothes, her furniture, and worst of all, her dioramas of her lost loves. Now both O'Connell women stand on the brink of rebuilding their futures.

Chris constructs a catapult by which he intends to hurl a cow through the air, thereby creating a perfect moment in performance art. The difficulty is finding the "right" cow. Joel expresses his displeasure at the animal cruelty associated with such an act, but Chris is determined in his quest. But when he finally finds the "right" cow, Ed tells him that Monty Python already catapulted a cow in their "Holy Grail" film. Not to be distracted from his pursuit of the perfect moment, Chris opts to hurl Maggie's scorched upright piano instead.

Meanwhile, Joel thinks he knows the local chimney sweep named Bob (guest star John M. Jackson), but he can't recall from where. Then he remembers: Bob is Larry Coe, one of Joel's golf idols who flubbed a perfect putt on the final hole of the Augusta National, and who had moved to Cicely to escape the shame of his links gaffe.

Written by Robin Green
Directed by Rob Thompson
Airdate: February 3, 1992

"DEMOCRACY IN AMERICA"

Log Line:

Mayoral incumbent Holling is stung by the news that he has a formidable opponent, old friend Edna Hancock, who's got a bee in her bonnet over a promise he never kept. The election also finds Shelly testing the aphrodisiac of power, Chris waxing patriotic, Ed anticipating his first time voting, and Joel and Maggie arguing party politics.

Synopsis:

Edna Hancock (guest star Rita Taggart) challenges Holling as mayor of Cicely, after waiting five years for him to put up a stop sign. Following twenty-three years as mayor, Holling is unseated 255 to 247.

Chris, a convicted felon who can't vote, thinks democracy in action is nirvana. In 1972, his Uncle Roy took him fishing at Little Spider Lake, until he remembered it was election day, Nixon versus McGovern. Uncle Roy was a Democrat, who'd been to Vietnam, and he hated Nixon. As a kid, Joel used to memorize election results and was probably the only Republican on the Upper West Side. Maggie's folks are pro-labor Democrats, and Ed discovers he has no views.

Maurice, who owns 15,000 acres around Cicely, realizes that now that Edna's let the genie out of the bottle, his dream of tract homes, shopping malls, and domed arenas will be ruined by bureaucrats, zoning boards and special interest groups—what he came to Cicely to escape.

Written by Jeff Melvoin
Directed by Michael Katleman
Airdate: February 24, 1992

"THREE AMIGOS"

Log Line:

The death of a rugged hunting companion sends Holling and Maurice into the wilderness to make good on a promise to bury him miles from civilization at a paradise called No-Name Point.

Synopsis:

Maurice and Holling's old hunting friend, Bill Planey, dies and, as promised, they aim to take old Bill's body to No-Name Point, along with Solvang (guest star Joanna Cassidy), Bill's headstrong wife of three winters. But old age yells louder than the Call of the Wild, and the boys lose more than their unhobbled horses, which they find in Two Forks, along with Reinhart Schoelder (guest star Norbert Weisser), Teak and Pig-Eye (guest star Tom Spiller), who fight Maurice and Holling over a bridge game. Solvang shacks up with Reinhart, also buying into his bar with the money Maurice and Holling gave her (Maurice writes a check for $1,643.81 and Holling kicks in a fifty). Holling and Maurice lose Bill's wrapped body down the river and end up burying him in a glen.

Written by Mitchell Burgess and Robin Green
Directed by Matthew Nodella
Airdate: March 2, 1992

"LOST AND FOUND"

Log Line:

Joel discovers his cabin is haunted, Eve is worried that she is suffering from an exotic illness, and Maurice is disappointed when his old friend from Korea turns out to be less than perfect.

Synopsis:

Joel hears a human-like sound inside his cabin one night. He mentions it to Ruth-Anne who tells him about Jack, a young man who committed suicide forty years before in Joel's cabin. To ease Joel's mind Maggie brings in an exorcist, but Joel refuses to let him work when he finds out Jack's soul may be doomed to hell because suicide is a mortal sin. Maggie tells Joel he identifies with Jack's situation as both are single, well-educated, thirtyish and cynical. But when Maggie points out that like Jack, Joel has no friends in Cicely and would never be mourned, he decides to invite everyone to a barbeque.

Eve, a well-known hypochondriac, appears in Joel's office insisting on a complete examination. Joel demands that she leave, because the last time they met she held him captive in her cabin for days. They eventually come to an understanding and Joel agrees to run a series of extensive tests on her. But when the results come back, Eve is surprised to learn that she isn't dying—but the rabbit has.

Maurice is excited because Gordon (guest star Noble Willingham), his former commanding officer in Korea, is coming to Cicely for a visit. Upon his arrival, Gordon asks Maurice to invest in a lodge he is building in Montana, which takes Maurice by surprise. Gordon later reveals he did not become an astronaut because he was disinterested but because he did not meet the qualifications, leaving Maurice to face the fact that his lifelong idol is not perfect.

Written by Diane Frolov and Andrew Schneider
Directed by Steve Robman
Airdate: March 9, 1992

"MY MOTHER, MY SISTER"

Log Line:

Shelly's mother drops in unexpectedly with her new twenty-four-year-old husband, a baby abandoned in Joel's waiting room is temporarily adopted by the townspeople, and Adam undergoes the same changes as his pregnant wife.

Synopsis:

Shelly's youthful mother, Tammy Tambo (guest star Wendy Schaal), visits unexpectedly to introduce her daughter to her new husband. Tammy admits that she has led her new love, twenty-four-year-old Kenny (guest star Sean O'Bryan), to believe that Shelly is Tammy's older sister. The two women have an argument and Tammy apologizes for not being a real mother to Shelly. Shelly realizes how lucky she is to have her mother as her best friend.

A baby abandoned in Joel's waiting room is immediately taken in by the townspeople. As it is passed from person to person, everyone is very delighted with the appearance of the child and, much to Joel's dismay, no one questions who the mother might be or why the baby was left. Just as the town is falling into a routine of caring for the infant, and as Joel finally accepts that she is there to stay, the baby is reclaimed by her mother.

When Joel compliments Adam on his cooking, he is shocked at Adam's congenial response. Confronted by Joel about this change in his personality, Adam explains that he doesn't feel like himself, he feels...happy. Joel suggests that he is suffering from Couvade Syndrome, sympathetic pregnancy, a condition in which men, in an attempt to mask their anxiety over their mate's pregnancy, displace their feelings with physical manifestations of pregnancy itself. The feelings eventually pass when Adam and Eve simultaneously enter their second trimester and Adam discovers he is more than just an extraordinary chef—he is also a husband, a teacher, a breadwinner, and soon, a father.

Written by Kate Boutilier and Mitchell Burgess
Directed by Rob Thompson
Airdate: March 16, 1992

"WAKE UP CALL"

Log Line:

The coming of spring brings love to Maggie, a new skin to Shelly and a reminder to Joel of the importance of blending compassion with his scientific knowledge.

Synopsis:

Maggie meets a tall, chiseled, almost animal-like stranger, when her truck becomes stuck in the slush. As the two get to know each other, Maggie becomes infatuated with Arthur (guest star Andreas Wisniewski), and is oblivious to his strange lifestyle which involves catching fish with his hands and living in a cave. Within a few days, Arthur brings flowers to Maggie and announces he must leave to join his family. After he departs, Maggie visits his cave only to find a very gentle bear who responds to the name of Arthur.

Leonard Quinhagak (guest star Graham Greene), Marilyn's cousin "the healer," observes Joel at work in order to expand his approach to medicine and be less holistic. He becomes involved when Shelly sees Joel because her skin is peeling. Leonard intervenes when Joel prescribes a medicated ointment that does not solve the problem. Leonard questions Shelly about her life, then diagnoses her skin is peeling because she is being reborn, just as a snake sloughs its skin. Leonard's accurate analysis reminds Joel of the importance of taking the feelings and the lifestyle of his patients into consideration when making a diagnosis.

Written by Diane Frolov and Andrew Schneider
Directed by Nick Marck
Airdate: March 23, 1992

"THE FINAL FRONTIER"

Log Line:

Much to Holling's dismay Ed discovers that Jesse the bear has died; Japanese tourists infiltrate Cicely; a package that has traveled the world arrives in Cicely addressed to an unknown person.

Synopsis:

Ed's announcement that Jesse the bear is dead affects Holling very personally. After having been attacked by Jesse years before, Holling had vowed to kill the bear himself someday. Jesse's death means an end to that dream. Refusing to accept the bear's demise, Holling sets off to the cave where Jesse lived. He returns cut and bruised, but finally at peace, having realized Jesse symbolized all fears and proud of himself for having faced them directly.

A group of Japanese people come to town to see the Aurora Borealis and to meet their hero, Maurice Minnifield the famed astronaut. Although flattered by the attention, Maurice becomes upset they are staying at the bed and breakfast that he sold to two gay men.

A package with postmarks from around the world arrives in Cicely, addressed to an unfamiliar name. After trying many different ways to contact this unknown person, the townspeople become curious about what the box contains. After arguing both sides, they vote to open it.

Written by Jeffrey Vlaming
Directed by Tom Moore
Airdate: April 27, 1992

"IT HAPPENED IN JUNEAU"

Log Line:

Things heat up between Joel and Maggie when they are forced to share a hotel room; Chris and his brother Bernard for the first time are not in perfect synch with each other.

Synopsis:

Joel excitedly waits for his plane to Juneau, where he is scheduled to speak at a medical conference, only to be disappointed that it is Maggie who will be flying him. Coincidentally, both have booked rooms at a hotel that has just experienced a burst pipe, making it impossible for the hotel to honor all of its reservations. Forced to share the last room in the hotel, a two bedroom suite, they agree to spend the weekend totally independent of each other. When Joel's presentation and his efforts to score with the female doctors are both unsuccessful, he finds himself alone with Maggie in the hotel room one evening and the feelings they have for each other finally erupt. Unbeknownst to Maggie, the night does not turn out quite the way they had anticipated.

Back in Cicely, the arrival of his brother Bernard influences Chris' speech pattern, making him unable to put words in a sensible order. For the first time ever the men are not on the same wavelength. Usually able to finish the other's sentences, they put their heads together to identify the cause for the deviation. After much thought they come to the conclusion Bernard's recent travels through Africa to explore his roots somehow caused him to lose synch with Chris. The discovery allows them to renew their connection.

Written by David Assael
Directed by Michael Katleman
Airdate: May 4, 1992

"OUR WEDDING"

Log Line:

Adam and Eve decide to wed for the baby's sake; Maggie avoids Joel like the plague, still believing that they slept together in Juneau; Officer Semanski serves Maurice with an official complaint.

Synopsis:

Although they have been living together for the last twelve years, Adam and Eve are not officially married. Now that Eve is six months pregnant, they decide they must legally wed for the sake of their child. The town becomes excited over the imminent celebration. Bachelor and bachelorette parties are thrown, the church is decorated, and the wedding attire gathered. All moves along smoothly until Eve begins walking down the aisle. Surprising everyone, she declares she cannot marry Adam because she is heiress to a large fortune. Chris' brother Bernard happens to be in town with a standard prenuptial agreement. After it is signed, the wedding proceeds as planned.

Throughout the week prior to the ceremony, Maggie avoids Joel like the plague. Still believing they slept together in Juneau, Maggie is embarrassed at the thought of it. When Joel finally tells her the truth, that she fell asleep before anything happened, she is disappointed that he did not want her badly enough to wake her up. To make herself feel better, Maggie stops by Joel's cabin

after the bachelorette party and announces she wants to have sex with him. Joel naturally complies, but as soon as things start to get hot, and Maggie is sure that he wants her, she leaves satisfied.

Officer Barbara Semanski delivers Maurice a formal complaint from the neighbor of a large piece of land he owns. The neighbor charges that when Maurice had his land excavated the explosion caused flying debris to hit and wound his grazing animals. The legal matter is quickly forgotten, but the chemistry between Semanski and Maurice remains apparent.

Written by Diane Frolov and Andrew Schneider
Directed by Nick Marck
Airdate: May 11, 1992

"CICELY"

Log Line:

Joel stumbles upon an elderly sage who tells him the story of Cicely's creation.

Synopsis:

While driving, Joel narrowly misses hitting an elderly man who he discovers is one of Cicely's first residents. In an ensuing conversation Ned (guest star Roberts Blossom) launches into an elaborate story about the creation of the town. As he speaks his words come to life on the screen.

The downtrodden town was run by Mace (Barry Corbin), an outlaw who controlled the inhabitants with an iron fist. It was when Mace left for a few months that Roslyn (guest star Jo Anderson), a powerful, robust woman, and Cicely (guest star Yvonne Suhor), a vision of grace and beauty, came to the village. Immediately Roslyn made an effort to clean up the town. She stood up for her beliefs and demanded civil and mannerly behavior. Roslyn took Ned (Darren E. Burrows), who was then a young man who lived like an animal and begged for food, and Sally (Cynthia Geary), a shamed hooker, under her wing and instilled in them a new sense of self esteem.

Together Roslyn and Cicely brought culture, peace, and open mindedness to the small community. The once primitive town came to appreciate such things as dance and poetry. Roslyn had created a place where everyone was accepted without prejudice. Franz Kafka (Rob Morrow) even visited the artist's utopia to alleviate his writer's block.

News that Mace was headed back to reclaim his town would jeopardize the now perfect society. Upon his entrance to town, Roslyn attempted to talk with him calmly on behalf of the townspeople. As she spoke with him, one of his gunmen fired.

After that day, the town and Roslyn were never the same.

Written by Diane Frolov and Andrew Schneider
Directed by Rob Thompson
Airdate: May 18, 1992

"NORTHWEST PASSAGES"

Log Line:

To celebrate her thirtieth birthday, Maggie spends the weekend camping alone to reflect on her life and cleanse her soul. Marilyn asks Chris to help her learn how to drive. Maurice rambles endlessly into a recorder about his past in an attempt to write his memoirs.

Synopsis:

Maggie decides that her thirtieth birthday is the perfect time to cleanse her soul so she can begin the next segment of her life with a clean slate. To do this she acts upon an ancient Indian ritual that allows one to resolve issues with people in one's past, living or dead, by sending them a letter via the great river. While camping alone and after "mailing" letters to all of her dead boyfriends, Maggie is overcome by a sharp pain and a high fever, which cause her to hallucinate. In her delirium she visits with all of her past boyfriends before being rescued and treated for appendicitis.

Chris is amazed by the fulfillment he derives from being a teacher when Marilyn asks him to give her driving lessons, Maurice takes a stab at writing his memoirs and drives everyone crazy with his neverending note-taking and muttering into a pocket recorder. Eventually Ruth-Anne takes charge and stops his madness.

Written by Robin Green
Directed by Dean Parisot
Airdate: September 28, 1992

"MIDNIGHT SUN"

Log Line:

Joel is "light loony" and, with his enormous amount of excess energy, coaches the Cicely Quarks in their annual basketball game against Sleetmute. An old friend drops in to visit Ruth-Anne and outfits the town from his collection of fashionable ensembles.

Synopsis:

Joel unknowingly becomes "light loony" during his first experience with twenty-four-hour sunlight. As a result, the usually dismal doctor is excessively happy and energetic. After not sleeping for days, he is amazed...that he is not even tired. When asked to coach the "Quarks," Cicely's town basketball team, he is thrilled to have a place to funnel his energy. "Coach" Fleischman gives the team everything he's got and more in an effort to beat Sleetmute in the annual game. Unfortunately, nature sees to it that Joel never has the opportunity to experience his moment of glory.

Gillis Toomey (guest star Jim Haynie), a traveling apparel salesman and old friend of Ruth-Anne's, visits Cicely for the first time in many years. The townspeople immediately welcome his return and are excited about shopping in his trailer full of wonderful garments. Gillis decides he would like to be more than a friend to Ruth-Anne and proposes marriage to her.

Written by Geoffrey Neigher
Directed by Michael Katleman
Airdate: October 5, 1992

"NOTHING'S PERFECT"

Log Line:

Chris kills a dog with his truck and quickly falls in love with its owner. Maurice buys an extremely expensive Augsburg clock and with its delivery comes a highly trained specialist to install it.

Synopsis:

Chris hits and kills a dog when it runs in front of his truck. He visits the address on the collar to apologize to its owners. When Amy Lochner (guest star Wendel Meldrum), a beautiful, intelligent woman, comes to the door, Chris is immediately intrigued and, after a few moments of conversation regarding her study of Pi and fondness for her many pets, they fall in love. When Chris accidentally kills a second pet, one of her parakeets, they decide that in order for their relationship to work it must be equal, thus he too must lose something he loves. Although painful for Chris, together they create the balance necessary.

Maurice's newly acquired ancient Augsburg clock is delivered to Cicely with a highly trained specialist, Rolf Hauser (guest star Mark Pellegrino), to install it. Although the clock is stunning, Maurice is disappointed it does not keep perfect time and demands a refund. Holling and Rolf help Maurice weigh the value of time versus the magnificence of this ancient relic.

Written by Diane Frolov and Andrew Schneider
Directed by Nick Marck
Airdate: October 12, 1992

"HEROES"

Log Line:

Chris must decide what to do with his deceased friend's remains. A heavy-metal rock star mistakenly arrives in Cicely instead of Sicily.

Synopsis:

Chris' longtime friend and mentor has his dead body sent to Chris. Faced with the dilemma of choosing the proper burial ritual for this great man, Chris contemplates everything from Egyptian mummifying to a traditional church service. After being reminded by Joel that time is of the essence in this situation, Chris finally decides upon a last rite that is worthy of his wise friend and personal hero.

Heavy-metal rock star, Brad Bonner (guest star Adam Ant), arrives in Cicely, Alaska instead of Sicily, Italy, his original destination, much to the delight of Shelly, one of his biggest fans. He quickly begins to enjoy the quiet and culture of Indian music. He enlists Ed to videotape his Alaskan adventures as he orchestrates a large concert which will blend the sound of two cultures. Unfortunately, in true Cicely style, things do not go as planned.

Written by Jeffrey Vlaming
Directed by Chuck Braverman
Airdate: October 19, 1992

"BLOWING BUBBLES"

Log Line:

A mysterious new resident quarantines himself in Cicely, arousing Maggie's interest and Joel's disbelief. Ruth-Anne must also cope with a new addition to the community—her materialistic son, Matthew, who gives up his career as an investment banker in Atlanta in search of a simpler life.

Synopsis:

An ex-lawyer from Chicago, Mike Monroe (guest star Anthony Edwards), moves into a geodesic dome in Cicely to seek relief from his multiple allergic reactions to the environment. His self-imposed quarantine in this plastic dome earns him the nickname of "Bubble Man" from the bemused residents, who experience varying reactions to Monroe's plight.

No one is more strongly drawn to the handsome Bubble Man than Maggie, however, who quickly develops a personal interest in Monroe's affliction. Joel is obligated to provide medical attention to Monroe and tells Maggie that Monroe is nuts—his acute allergies are merely psychosomatic.

Ruth-Anne receives an unexpected visit from another newcomer. Her investment-banker son, Matthew (guest star Joel Polis), moves in after losing his job in Atlanta. He assures his mother he has given up his materialistic lifestyle and is a changed man. To Ruth-Anne's dismay, Matthew wants to relocate to Cicely and open a tackle shop.

But Maurice has other plans for the hotshot investment whiz: Spaceship Cicely, a planned community of luxury condos for the environmentally stricken.

Written by Mark Perry
Directed by Rob Thompson
Airdate: November 2, 1992

"ON YOUR OWN"

Log Line:

The Flying Man returns to Cicely to woo Marilyn; Ed finds a ring that once belonged to Federico Fellini; Maurice has Mike rewrite his will to include his recently discovered Korean son, Duk Won.

Synopsis:

The Flying Man, Enrico Bellati, who fell in love with Marilyn while traveling through Cicely with the circus last year, returns. Now with a group of Mummenschanz, Bellati, temporarily grounded with a broken leg, proclaims his love for Marilyn. Although Marilyn admits her feelings for him, she refuses to leave her home to join him in his travels.

Ed, unable to finish his movie due to a mind block, finds a ring which once belonged to the great film director, Federico Fellini, and is inspired by it.

When Maurice receives a package from his newly discovered Korean son, Duk Won, he is reminded that he must include Duk Won in his will....

Maurice asks Mike Monroe, the only lawyer in town, to rewrite it for him. Maggie volunteers to act as Mike's legal secretary until things between them become too close for comfort.

Written by Sy Rosen and Christian Williams
Directed by Joan Tewksbury
Airdate: November 9, 1992

"THE BAD SEED"

Log Line:

Everyone is shocked when Holling's unknown illegitimate daughter arrives in town—especially Holling who believed he was sterile. Maggie assists Marilyn in her search for her dream house. Ed is excited about his annual visit from Princess, a crane he took under his wing when she was abandoned as a baby.

Synopsis:

Jackie Vincoeur (guest star Valerie Perrine), a swindler by nature, arrives in town and announces she is Holling's daughter. Holling is even more shocked than the rest of the townspeople, having believed he was sterile due to a childhood case of the mumps. Knowing the Vincoeurs are a bad lot, that they are vicious, cruel people, Holling is worried that the family line will not end with him as he had planned.

Unfortunately, Jackie lives up to the Vincoeur family name. She is immediately a bad influence on Shelly, encouraging her to drink, smoke and gamble. The unscrupulous Jackie cheats and takes advantage of anyone who crosses her path. True to her character, she admits to Holling the only reason she tracked him down was to coerce him into giving her money.

Marilyn moves out of her mother's house because she's tired of always living by mother's rules and asks Maggie to help her find a house to buy. After showing Marilyn numerous homes, Maggie finally finds Marilyn's dream house. In the meantime, Marilyn's mother (guest star Armenia Miles) puts her house on the market, because without her daughter living there she doesn't need such a big place. Marilyn buys it and invites her mother to live there but only under her own rules.

Ed is excited to see Princess, a crane he nurtured when she was abandoned as a baby, on her annual pass through Cicely. He notices she is the only one in the flock without a mate and teaches her how to find one.

Written by Mitchell Burgess
Directed by Randall Miller
Airdate: November 16, 1992

"THANKSGIVING"

Log Line:

Cicely readies itself for the annual Day of the Dead parade and Thanksgiving Day feast; Joel discovers he owes the state of Alaska a fifth year of service.

Synopsis:

The Indians celebrate Thanksgiving as the Day of the Dead with various traditions including costumes, parades and throwing tomatoes at white people. As all of the townspeople join in preparing for the festivities, Chris reflects upon the best Thanksgiving he ever had, which he experienced while in the State Penitentiary.

Joel receives a letter from the State of Alaska stating that he owes them a fifth year of service. He immediately brings the letter and the original contract to Mike Monroe for his legal advice. The contract, executed in 1986, stated that, at that time four years worth of work was equal to the cost of Joel's medical school tuition. Since that time, the value of the dollar has decreased, thus Joel now owes another year. The thought of being forced to stay in Cicely a year more than he anticipated depresses Joel to the point that the celebration going on around him cannot raise his spirits.

Written by David Assael
Directed by Michael Fresco
Airdate: November 23, 1992

"DO THE RIGHT THING"

Log Line:

An ex-member of the KGB visits Cicely to sell Maurice his official Russian dossier; a health inspector surveys The Brick for the first time in more then thirty years; Maggie makes a vow to herself to live each day as if it was her last.

Synopsis:

Viktor (guest star David Hemmings), an ex-Russian spy, arrives in town to sell Maurice his official dossier prepared by the Russian government. Since Maurice is in the midst of writing his memoirs, he purchases the file. Upon reading the information, he discovers the KGB knew of the one time he breached security. Chris helps him deal with his guilt by making him realize that everyone makes mistakes, even General MacArthur.

Viktor barters with Joel—a badly needed medical examination in exchange for the dossier of Yevgeny Fleischman, a possible, although highly unlikely, relative of Joel's. As the doctor pours over the file, he becomes immersed in Yevgeny's life.

Jason (guest star John Hawkes), a young health inspector, visits The Brick for the first time since 1959. Holling takes personal offense at being told how to run his business. Realizing the importance of the inspection, Holling goes so far as to send Shelly to the movies with the young official in an attempt to achieve a higher grade.

When a neighboring pilot dies in a plane crash, Maggie becomes preoccupied with death and decides to live each day as if it was her last. Eventually the stress of constantly being a generous, loving, kind person causes her to begin developing an ulcer.

Written by Diane Frolov and Andrew Schneider
Directed by Nick Marck
Airdate: November 30, 1992

"CRIME AND PUNISHMENT"

Log Line:

Chris' past finally catches up with him and he is apprehended and tried for breaking parole in the state of West Virginia many years earlier.

Synopsis:

When Chris-in-the-Morning is suddenly arrested for breaking parole many years before by leaving West Virginia without the consent of his parole officer, the townspeople immediately come to his aid. Maurice hires Mike to defend Chris. Mike, who was formerly a corporate attorney, is challenged to find a solid defense for Chris. After having everyone testify to the good person that Chris has become and painting the picture of his dysfunctional childhood, Mike attempts to prove the Chris Stevens currently before the court is not the same Chris Stevens who hot-wired a car at the tender age of eighteen.

Written by Jeff Melvoin
Directed by Rob Thompson
Airdate: December 14, 1992

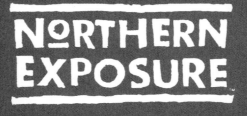

THE SOUNDS
OF CICELY

K-BEAR, Arrowhead County's favorite (and, apparently, only) radio station, may have the most eclectic playlist in North America, and, thanks to the magic of TV, the jukebox in Holling's bar seems to have an inexhaustible supply of CDs, as well.

Where does all that music come from? Much of it comes from co-creator Josh Brand, according to co-producer Mark Bruestle, who can cite several examples of Brand hearing a street musician or a catchy tune played in a restaurant and calling with instructions to Find That Tune.

The *Northern Exposure* sound track ranges easily from grand opera to gritty rock 'n' roll, often within the same episode.

"It's a lot of needle-dropping," says Bruestle. "It's really important to play the [prospective] music with the picture."

Music has evolved into an integral element of the Cicely sensibility. There are two types of Cicely sounds: "underscore," which is music playing while something else is going on, and "source music," which is music ostensibly emanating from a "source," such as Holling's jukebox or a radio tuned to K-BEAR.

"We came to think of music as sort of the sixth man on the show, our John Havlicek," Josh Brand, who's fond of sports metaphors, has said. "We use music to change the quality of scenes on the show, and we have used it to get us out of situations. It makes things that don't work *work* and things that do work, work better."

Examples abound. Take "Spring Break," the season-ending episode that climaxed with the Running of the Bulls, Cicely's infamous annual males-only nude run:

As the nude runners are filmed in long shot, "all the women from the town are cheering on the street," recalls Bruestle. "What we did is, we killed all the sound of the women screaming and didn't play any sounds and just played this song."

The song was "D.W. Suite," written by Lindsay Buckingham after Beach Boy Dennis Wilson drowned. "It's a song about going crazy," adds Bruestle. "And it was just very peaceful. Instead of playing the women screaming and shouting, we establish that in the first five seconds that they were screaming and shouting, and then it disappeared and it brought a different element.... That's where music can really elevate a scene and bring on a quality that doesn't [otherwise] exist."

So successful has the eclectic Cicely sound become that the producers have fielded thousands of requests from fans wanting information on a particular snippet of song. And, yes, they do listen to unsolicited music that comes over the transom; and, yes, they do use it too.

What follows are lists of all music played in the first four seasons through the end of 1992.

SUMMER 1990 SEASON

PILOT

Louie, Louie RICHARD BERRY
Joel meets Ed, who gives him a ride into town in his truck.

Family Tradition HANK WILLIAMS, JR.
Joel bursts into the Brick, and promptly makes a phone call to say that he wants out of his contract.

Truly Do BUD AND TRAVIS
Joel sits at the bar and talks to Holling and Ed.

Jolie Louise DANIEL LANOIS
Joel hears Holling's story of the feud between him and Maurice.

Get Your Life LIVINGSTON
Maggie and Joel meet, and Joel mistakenly assumes she is a prostitute.

Good Golly, Miss Molly
Barbeque montage.

Singing the Blues
Joel and Ed eat mooseburgers at the barbeque.

"BRAINS, KNOW-HOW AND NATIVE INTELLIGENCE"

Another Op'nin', Another Show Kiss Me Kate cast recording
Maurice on the mike, Joel takes a shower.

March of the Siamese Children The King and I cast recording
Joel looks for a book on plumbing in Ruth-Anne's store.

This Was a Real Nice Clambake Carousel cast recording
Joel and Ed talk as Joel attempts to fix his shower.

Wunderbar Kiss Me Kate cast recording
Joel examines Maggie's trick knee.

"SOAPY SANDERSON"

Unity
Ed delivers a note from Soapy to Joel.

Honky Tonk Angels KITTY WELLS
Joel and Maggie discuss their joint inheritance.

Knoxville Girl WILBURN BROS.
Joel calls Elaine from the Brick. Maggie introduces students making a documentary.

I Wanna Be a Cowboy Sweetheart PATSY MONTANA
Joel eats at the bar.

Take an Old Cold Tater and Wait LITTLE JIMMY DICKENS
Joel asks Chris how he should apologize to Maggie.

"DREAMS, SCHEMES AND PUTTING GREENS"

Overture to The Mikado
Maurice takes Japanese businessmen for a drive.

Diet of Strange Places K. D. LANG
Holling proposes to Shelly.

Get Your Life
Holling meets Shelly's dad.

My Way
Shelly is stood up at the altar.

Honky Tonk Angels KITTY WELLS
An enraged Shelly hurls drinking glasses at Holling.

Sukiyaki SAKAMOTO
Joel happily walks along the golf course.

Hello Young Lovers The King and I cast recording
Maurice sings at Shelly and Holling's wedding.

Just Like You
Outdoor shot of Cicely, closing scene.

"THE RUSSIAN FLU"

Who Put the Bomp (in the Bomp Bomp Bomp) BARRY MANN
An unusually spry Joel prepares for his girlfriend's visit.

On Broadway THE DRIFTERS
Joel asks Maggie to pick up Elaine in Anchorage.

New York, New York GRAND MASTER FLASH
Montage of outdoor shots.

Let's Dance BENNY GOODMAN
Dream sequence in which Joel dreams he is married to Maggie.

Stand by Me BEN E. KING
Maurice extols Joel for curing everyone's flu.

"SEX, LIES AND ED'S TAPES"

Lady Be Good DJANGO REINHARDT
Shelly tells Holling of her past with Wayne.

The Girl From Ipanema
Wayne tells Holling of his history with Shelly.

Little Girl Eyes ROBBIN JULIEN
Wayne and Shelly share a tender moment.

Without You MOTLEY CRUE
Shelly and Wayne reminisce as they dance to "their song."

Twilight Zone Theme
Rick hums this in Joel's office.

Ragtime Roy
Ed's daydream—an oldtime Western fight.

I'll See You in My Dreams GIANT
Shelly tells Wayne she does not love him anymore.

A Kiss to Build a Dream On LOUIS ARMSTRONG
Shelly and Holling make up as she massages his stiff neck.

This Land Is Your Land
The townsfolk sing as they await Ed's presentation.

"A KODIAK MOMENT"

Stardust
Maggie delivers a box of bagels to Joel.

Rhinestone Cowboy GLEN CAMPBELL
Maurice tells Chris that his brother Malcom died.

Caro, Nome
Maurice asks Chris to be his son.

Daddy's Home SHEP & THE LIMELIGHTS
Chris and a woman in the backseat of Maurice's car.

"THE AURORA BOREALIS"

Moon River LOUIS ARMSTRONG
Opening scene, Chris on the microphone. Closing scene, Chris and Bernard
look at Aurora Borealis.

Moonlight Sonata
Ed and Joel see Adam's footprint.

Bad Moon Rising CCR
Bernard enters Cicely on his motorcycle.

Little Egypt THE COASTERS
Joel stops driving his truck when he sees a ranger.

Blue Moon BILLIE HOLIDAY
Chris and Bernard, both on the same wavelength, clean up in a game of bridge.

Mr. Sandman THE CHORDETTES
Dream sequence where Chris and Bernard share the same dream.

Full Moon, Full of Love K. D. LANG
Joel announces that he has seen Adam.

SPRING 1991 SEASON

"GOODBYE TO ALL THAT"

Stardust
Joel and Maggie argue as they discuss her bladder infection.

R.B. Blues RUTH BROWN
Joel and Chris talk about relationships.

Down Hearted Blues MILDRED BAILEY
A desperate Shelly drinks coffee as she becomes addicted to TV.

Guitars, Cadillacs DWIGHT YOAKAM
Joel, Chris, and Joel's blind date play pool. Shelly dresses like Vanna White.

One Foot Draggin' THE COASTERS
Joel's blind date leaves him.

It's Just a Girl Thang ICEY J
Shelly dances on the bar as she continues to watch TV.

Let's Dance BENNY GOODMAN
Joel daydreams that he stops Elaine from marrying the older man.

Tea With Alice
Joel and Ed talk about closure.

Lulu
Shelly is glued to the TV. Ed tells the gang that Joel needs closure.

Magnum P.I. Theme
Shelly recites a full lineup of TV shows.

Get Your Life
Holling serves drinks to Maggie and Joel.

Blue Moon BILLIE HOLIDAY
Shelly apologizes to Holling.

"THE BIG KISS"

Closings #4
Ed watches TV.

She is Not Thinking of Me LOUIS JOURDAN
Chris is taken with a beautiful woman and loses his voice.

Ya Ya LEE DORSEY
Ed brings "One Who Waits" to the Brick.

Mambo Baby RUTH BROWN
Holling and Maurice talk to Chris.

Truly Do BUD AND TRAVIS
Maurice tells a tale of a woman who stole a man's courage.

Let the Tear Drops Fall
Maggie talks to Chris in the Brick.

Pretty Lady
Pacific Overtures cast recording
Maurice daydreams of Shelly's beauty pageant.

Weiner Cafe
Joel and Maurice talk about the effects of women.

Tea With Alice
Maggie has dinner with Chris.

Reach Out and Touch
Maggie tells Joel of her dinner date with Chris.

La Mer CHARLES TRENET
Chris arrives at Maggie's house in hopes of getting his voice back.

Honeysuckle Rose DJANGO REINHARDT AND STEPHANE GRAPPELLI
Maurice and Shelly talk about their first meeting.

Third Man Theme ANTON KARAS
Joel asks Chris about his evening with Maggie.

When I Grow Too Old to Dream NAT KING COLE
Ed helps a stranger (could be his father) change his truck tire.

"ALL IS VANITY"

Honky Tonk Angels KITTY WELLS
An argument breaks out in the Brick about hunting dogs.

Bon Soir Dame BUD AND TRAVIS
Holling tells Shelly that he talked to Joel about getting circumsized.

Saturday Night Is the Loneliest Night of the Week ROSEMARY CLOONEY
Holling tells Joel that he wants the operation.

Angie (from *Wild Is the Wind*)
Holling has circumcision dream.

Symphony No. 7 (BEETHOVEN)
Chris on the microphone.

Tradition
Maggie tells Joel that her father thinks she and Joel are dating.

If I Were a Rich Man
Chris dedicates song to Holling.

Diet of Strange Places K. D. LANG
Holling is edgy about his upcoming operation.

"WHAT I DID FOR LOVE"

The Sunshine of Love LOUIS ARMSTRONG
Ingrid, Maurice's old flame, comes to town.

Overture *The King and I* cast recording
Maurice and Ingrid in bed.

Buck's Neuvelle Jole Blon BUCKWHEAT ZYDECO
Ed tries to persuade Joel to sell his plane ticket.

I'm in Love With a Wonderful Guy *South Pacific* cast recording
Joel daydreams what Cicely would be like without him.

On the Street Where You Live and *I Could Have Danced All Night*
My Fair Lady cast recording
Ingrid tells Maurice that he stops breathing in his sleep.

I'm a Little Teapot
Dave sings with the children.

Lullaby MAUREEN FORRESTER
Joel daydreams about his upcoming flight.

You Do Something to Me SINEAD O'CONNOR
Maggie dances around her apartment.

"SPRING BREAK"

D.W. Suite LINDSEY BUCKINGHAM
Opening scene—outdoor shots of snowy Cicely. Closing scene—
men of Cicely streak through town.

Crazy PATSY CLINE
Joel picks up a lingerie magazine in Ruth-Anne's store.

Big Bad Bill LEON REDBONE
Holling is itching for a fight. Ed announces Joel's radio was stolen.

Simply Irresistible ROBERT PALMER
Joel's Robert Palmer dream.

Bon Soir Dame BUD AND TRAVIS
Maurice announces his boom box was stolen.

El Cajon STAN GETZ
Chris on the microphone reads from a children's book.

Everybody be Yo Self CHIC STREETMAN
Party atmosphere in the Brick. Maggie and Joel kiss passionately in the kitchen.

Aria from Diva
Diva soundtrack recording
Ed confronts Chris about the items he stole.

Tea With Alice
Joel and Maggie confess that they've been fantasizing about each other.

"WAR AND PEACE"

I Don't Care HANK WILLIAMS
Holling blows up at Dave.

Love Is a Many-Splendored Thing JOHN WILLIAMS
Ed stops Father Duncan from driving away and meets Lightfeather.

Internationale
Chris talks on the radio.

Pictures at an Exhibition (MUSSORGSKY)
The chess game.

Romeo and Juliet (TCHAIKOVSKY)
Ed stays for supper.

One More Kiss Dear *Blade Runner* sound track recording
Lightfeather comes on to Chris.

Lara's Theme *Doctor Zhivago* sound track
Nikolai and Maurice duel.

What'll I Do? IRVING BERLIN
Nikolai sings.

"SLOW DANCE"

Willow Tree ALTON AND HORTENSE ELLIS
Maggie and Rick quarrel about his pilot license.

Sugarmoon K. D. LANG
Shelly meets Holling's lady friend, Anita.

Fools Paradise CHARLES BROWN
Joel tells Maggie that Rick is dead.

Oh! What a Beautiful Mornin' *Oklahoma* cast recording
Maurice has dinner with Ron and Eric.

Pathique (BEETHOVEN)
A neighbor brings Maggie cookies and makes a pass at her.

Reach Out and Touch
Maurice defends his heterosexuality.

Is That All There Is PEGGY LEE
Rick's funeral service.

Juliet of the Spirits
Pallbearers carry Rick's coffin.

Song from Moulin Rouge PERCY FAITH
Shelly, dressed like an old woman, serves dinner to Holling.

Let the Teardrops Fall
Shelly and Holling discuss their age difference.

Mambo Baby RUTH BROWN
Joel consoles Maggie while discussing her bad luck with men.

At Last ETTA JAMES
Joel and Maggie dance.

1991/92 SEASON

"THE BUMPY ROAD TO LOVE"

Bon Soir Dame BUD AND TRAVIS
Joanne and Maggie talk in bar about Rick.

Sonata in D Moll (SCARLATTI)
Maurice, Semanski, Holling and Shelly have dinner at Maurice's.

Don't Let That Man Get You Down TEXAS RUBY
Maggie talks to Ed about men at the bar.

Mana'O Pili DIANA AKI
Maurice comes to KBHR to talk about Semanski with Chris.

I Feel Better All Over FERLIN HUSKY
Maggie continues to talk to Ed. Ruth Anne arrives to take Maggie home.

"ONLY YOU"

I'm In The Mood for Love BILL COLEMAN
Maggie asks Joel if there is anything she can do about her eyes—"Basset hound" scene.

Laredo Rose TEXAS TORNADOS
Maurice and Holling have argument over picture and Shelly.

I Want to be Sedated RAMONES
Joel comes to Chris's trailer—it is surrounded by women. Joel tells him about pheromones.

Tea With Alice
Irene examines elderly man. Chris enters and asks her if she can smell him.

Let's Dream in the Moonlight BILLIE HOLIDAY
Chris and Maurice talk about women in radio station.

Under the Stormy Sky DANIEL LANOIS
Maggie shows up wearing makeup; Shelly starts to explain her version of the "love triangle."

Tea With Alice
Chris tells Joel that he's in love with Irene; Chris and Irene talk in front of van.

Tea With Alice
Chris and Joel talk—his attraction has ended. Chris and Irene talk (folding chair scene).

I'll Try Again KELLY WILLIS
Joel and Maggie talk. Maggie borrows Joel's glasses, and Maurice enters bar.

Let's Dream in the Moonlight BILLIE HOLIDAY
Chris talks on the radio as he watches Optomobile leave town.

"OY WILDERNESS"

Layin' Back
Cyndy arrives at Holling's bar.

Can't Stop Lovin' You CHET ATKINS
Holling and Cyndy talk about dating and marriage.

Celito Lindo
Joel cooks and tries to eat liver.

Love Song TESLA
Cyndy gives Marilyn a manicure; Cyndy and Shelly fight in bathroom.

Love Is a Hard Game to Play STEVIE NICKS
Shelly and Cyndy talk on the bed and make up.

I'll See You in My Dreams JAN GARBER
Holling talks to Chris about Shelly at radio station.

Party Night UNDIVIDED ROOTS
Shelly and Cyndy ask Chris to perform radio divorce.

Amazing Grace
Chris performs radio divorce.

Love Is a Hard Game to Play STEVIE NICKS
Shelly and Cyndy say goodbye; Shelly and Holling snuggle in bed.

"ANIMALS R US"

Time Changes Everything BOB WILLS AND THE TEXAS PLAYBOYS
Dog eats beef jerky; sits on Rick's bar stool.

Pathetique (BEETHOVEN)
Maggie fixes dog dinner, asks if he is Rick.

Flute Quartet—Alegretto (KROMER)
Maurice and Marilyn talk ostrich business over dinner.

My Reason for Living FERLIN HUSKY

Gotta Travel On CHET ATKINS
Maggie tells everyone the dog is Rick.

Praeludium from Partita #1 B-Major (BACH)*
Ed watches Marilyn and Maurice walk down the street.

My Boyfriend's Back THE ANGELS
Maggie throws the dog out after she finds herself waiting on him.

Praeludium from Partita #1 B-Major (BACH)*
Ed films the town.

Natural Woman ARETHA FRANKLIN
Maggie and the dog frolic in the park.

Hip, Hug, Her BOOKER T AND THE MGs
Maggie arrives at the bar after her picnic—accuses Joel of being jealous of the dog.

One More Kiss Dear *Blade Runner* sound track recording
Marilyn tells Maurice deal is off; Maurice enter bar; he and Joel talk. He asks if he's a nice
guy. Joel asks why animals don't like him.

Praeludium from Partita #1 B-Major (BACH)*
Ed's movie.

*adapted by David Schwartz, *Northern Exposure* composer.

"JULES ET JOEL"

Flight of the Cosmic Hippo BELA FLECK AND THE FLECKTONES
Joel makes dinner and Frank arrives. Jules arrives in Cicely.

I Heard the Jukebox Playing KITTY WELLS
Maggie talks to Shelly about Joel; Joel discovers that Jules is in town.

I Wanna Be a Cowboy Sweetheart DIXIE CHICKS
Jules, Maurice and Ed talk in Holling's. Jules and Ed leave.

Don Quichote MAGAZINE 60
Ed tells Joel he knows he's not Jules. "Jules" asks Maggie what she thinks of Joel.

Mo Onions BOOKER T AND THE MGs
Frank tells Chris to meet him in the woods.

Don Quichote MAGAZINE 60
Maurice and Semanski arrive. Semanski arrests Joel.

Flight of the Cosmic Hippo BELA FLECK AND THE FLECKTONES
Joel's put in jail. He talks with Freud.

Summertime BOOKER T AND THE MGs
Ed and Chris in radio station; Frank calls.

All the Way LEE MORGAN
Maggie and Jules talk, kiss.

Flight of the Cosmic Hippo BELA FLECK AND THE FLECKTONES
Freud falls asleep on Joel.

Minuet (BOCCHERINI)
Maggie and Joel have dinner.

"THE BODY IN QUESTION"

La Donna A Mobile
While fishing, Chris finds a frozen body.

Rue St. Michael
Chris and Shelly talk about Napoleon at Holling's.

Jolie Louise DANIEL LANOIS
Maggie reads from journal—Napoleon's wife is pregnant. Joel gets piece of
Pierre's jacket for testing.

I Got You DWIGHT YOAKAM
Holling tells Joel about his mean genes.

Hot Club Hop
Shelly discovers that Pierre has been stolen.

"ROOTS"

Poor Boy Blues CHET ATKINS AND MARK KNOPFLER
Bernard offers Chris a check from Dad.

Wild Side of Life HANK THOMPSON
Holling's bar—Joel broods about Elaine, while Adam makes bet with Holling.

I'm Blue Again PATSY CLINE
Maggie and Shelly have discussion about Elaine's motives in coming to see Joel.

Dede Priscilla LEA LIGNANZI

Caballo Viejo ROBERT TORRES
Adam advised Chris and Bernard on restaurants. Joel and Elaine have conversation at Holling's.

Beale Street Mama CAB CALLOWAY
Holling pays Adam for winning the bet.

Emabhaceni MIRIAM MAKEBA
Bernard leaves Cicely, while Maggie and Joel walk down street.

"A-HUNTING WE WILL GO"

Layin' Back
Holling and Chris talk about going hunting. Joel joins them in discussion and ends up wanting to join the hunting trip.

Again Tonight JOHN MELLENCAMP
Shelly and Ed talk about Ruth-Anne's age at Holling's.

It's All About to Change TRAVIS TRITT
Shelly tells the story about taking her fish for a walk; Ed's looking for ideas for Ruth-Anne's gift; Maggie can't believe Joel actually shot a bird.

Black Orchid PETER MOON BAND
Joel sadly announces the bird has died. Shelly serves him cornflakes for breakfast after Holling has suggested eggs.

"GET REAL"

Grand River BYRON DERLINE
Chris and Steven talk about darts and physics. Holling notices how large Shelly's feet are.

Little Girl Eyes ROBIN JULIEN
Holling asks Shelly to marry him—she knows he's up to something.

Bolero CIRQUE DU SOLEIL
The troupe performs for the town. Bellati performs for Marilyn.

Little Ways DWIGHT YOAKAM

The Sweetest Thing CARLENE CARTER
Adrienne reads Maggie's palm at Holling's.

"SEOUL MATES"

Santa Claus Is Coming to Town BOOKER T. AND THE MGs
Chris whittles the raven; Maurice comes in depressed. Maurice's family comes to town.

Dig That Crazy Santa Claus OSCAR MCLOLLIE AND THE HONEY JUMPERS
Ed and Dave bring in tree. Maggie enters and trips. Joel tells Maggie to tell her parents she's too busy to go home for Christmas.

Il Est Ne/Ca Berger THE CHIEFTANS

Shelly's bummed, tells Holling she misses a "real" Christmas.

Christmas Time's a Coming PETER ROLOAN

Maurice talks to his family at Holling's. He thinks they have an ulterior motive.

Silent Night

Maggie gets letter from her parents. They're headed to St. Thomas for the holidays.

Fly Me to the Moon

Maurice's son sings to him at dinner.

White Christmas ALLEN TOUSSAINT

Shelly plays with the manger scene, while Maggie convinces herself she'll have a good Christmas. Dave introduces his parents.

O Come All Ye Faithful THE CHIEFTANS

The Christmas Song TONY BENNETT

Maurice and his son talk at Hollings. Maurice is delighted he's an engineer. They arm wrestle.

White Christmas CLYDE MCPHATTER AND THE DRIFTERS

Joel invites Maggie over to help decorate his tree, but she's not in the Christmas spirit.

Ave Maria (SCHUBERT)

Holling sings to Shelly.

"DATELINE: CICELY"

Blues for Your Own SALLY VAN METER
Joel discovers Adam in the kitchen teaching Dave. Adam tells Joel that Eve is sick (as usual).

Please Don't Let Me Love You ROBERT MORGAN
Maurice enters Holling's—announces that his newspaper has been abused and he's sick of it.

Pussy Cat
Holling and Chris make deal on the Brick.

Madeliena PABLO LUBADIKA PORTHOS
Shelly and Adam serve food. Ed and Maurice talk about Ed's new idea for a movie review column.

Nou Pop Sa Blize BOUKMAN EKSPERYANS
Maggie tries explaining to Joel how trees communicate.

Layin' Back
Chris tells Holling that he thinks he should do something with the moosehead on the wall.

Stormy Weather*
Chris on the radio—talks about changing the things you love.

Guitar Rag
Maurice looks for Adam at Holling's.

Stormy Weather*
Joel tries to cheer up Maurice. Ed enters with newspaper about trees crying.

*adapted by David Schwartz

"OUR TRIBE"

On Monday RED KNUCKLES AND THE TRAILBLAZERS
Ruth-Anne and Holling talk about waxing the floors.

Going Steady RED KNUCKLES AND THE TRAILBLAZERS
Holling kicks everyone out of the bar.

On the Alamo BENNY GOODMAN SEXTET
Joel and Marilyn talk on the street.

The Sky Fell Down TOMMY DORSEY
Joel goes to Ruth-Anne's. Everyone is waiting in line for coffee since Holling's is closed.

Honey Babe RED CLAY RAMBLERS
Joel enters his office. The town has transformed his office into a makeshift Holling's.

Blue Interlude ARTIE SHAW
Holling tells Maggie about his star charts and "Eleanor."

Mood Indigo DUKE ELLINGTON
Chris on the radio—he's bummed about Holling's being closed. Maurice tries to cheer him up.

"THINGS BECOME EXTINCT"

I Love You a Thousand Ways TIM AND MOLLIE O'BRIAN
Ed looks for something to film for his project.

Tea Dance
Ira brings his flutes to Ruth-Anne's store.

Memories of You BENNY GOODMAN
Ed and Ira talk about Ed filming the making of duck flutes.

Someone Took My Place With You DAVID PARMLEY
Holling talks to Shelly as he goes through a box of old things.

Family Traditions HANK WILLIAMS, JR.
Joel and Ed talk in Joel's cabin.

Sleepy Steel

Acapulco Serenata
Shelly performs a puppet show for Holling.

"BURNING DOWN THE HOUSE"

The Prisoner's Song VERNON DALHART
Maggie buys supplies for her Mom at Ruth-Anne's store.

Whispering PAUL WHITEMAN
Chris and Shelly talk about art and catapults.

Fell in Love TIM O'BRIEN
Mrs. O'Connell tells Maggie she is divorcing Mr. O'Connell.

Roses and Midnight
Joel picks up his *Golf Digest* and realizes who Bob really is.

Sweetest Things CARLENE CARTER
Maggie and Holling talk about happiness.

A Little Unfair BRENDA LEE

Where Would That Leave Me?
Holling, Shelly, Maurice, and Joel talk in Holling's bar.

The Blue Danube (J. STRAUSS)
The piano is flung!

"DEMOCRACY IN AMERICA"

J'ai Fait Une Grosse Error (I Made a Big Mistake) JIMMY NEWMAN
Edna challenges Holling to an election.

Fanfare for the Common Man (AARON COPLAND)
Chris announces the political race over the airwaves.

Guitar Boogie ARTHUR SMITH
Joel and Ed talk about voting.

Stars and Stripes Forever
Joel and Ruth-Anne listen to Chris on the radio.

America the Beautiful AMERICAN BOYS CHOIR
Chris talks on the radio.

The Hobo DOC WATSON
Edna stops Holling from giving away free beer.

Appalachian Spring (AARON COPLAND)
Maggie and Joel let people in the church to vote.

Crazy MIKE AULDRIDGE
Holling tells people to stop moping.

This Is My Country AMERICAN BOYS CHOIR
End of the show

"THREE AMIGOS"

It Won't Hurt DWIGHT YOAKAM
Maurice brings news of Bill's death.

Grand River
Maurice buys supplies for his trip.

The Whiskey Ain't Working
Maurice and Holling sit by the campfire.

Acoustic Duet 1 COUNTRY BLUES GUITAR
Maurice and Holling play cards.

Hands on the Wheel WILLIE NELSON
Shelly gives Holling a bath.

"LOST AND FOUND"

Sin Ti BUD AND TRAVIS
Joel finds out about Jack.

Again Tonight JOHN MELLENCAMP
Maggie works on her car and talks to Joel about Jack.

Side by Side KAY STARR
Maurice introduces the Colonel to everyone in the bar.

Terrible Thing BOOKER T. AND THE MGs
Chris talks about a brick.

Mein Herr Marquis
Eve and Ruth-Anne talk about antacids.

"MY MOTHER, MY SISTER"

A Woman Half My Age KITTY WELLS
Adam talks about food preparation, and hurts Dave's feelings.

Laid Back

Sleepy Steel
Tammy walks into the bar.

Gimme Three Steps LYNARD SKYNARD
Tammy dances in Holling's bar.

Viola Concerto

Scherzo
Adam and Ruth-Anne chat.

Diet of Strange Places K.D. LANG
Holling serves Kenny a beer.

Shame, Shame, Shame JOHNNY WINTERS
Holling, Shelly, Tammy, and Kenny have dinner in Holling's bar.

Paradise City GUNS 'N ROSES
Tammy tells the others about meeting Slash.

Blue Sky THE ALLMAN BROTHERS

I Could Never Live Without You ENUFF Z NUFF

Blue Sky THE ALLMAN BROTHERS
Shelly and Tammy talk in Shelly's bedroom.

Too Weak to Fight JOHNNY LAW

Hot Club Stomp

I Believe in Steel
Tammy and Kenny say their goodbyes.

Gimme Three Steps LYNARD SKYNARD
Shelly gives Holling a bath.

"WAKE UP CALL"

Guitars and Cadillacs DWIGHT YOAKAM
Maurice decorates The Brick with geraniums.

Invention #8 (BACH)
Chris talks on the radio.

Musette Madeline
Maggie laments about not having a man.

Imperial Hotel
Shelly is peeling.

Music Hall Waltz
Leonard talks to Joel.

Bailero FREDRICA VON STAADE
Maggie and Arthur dance in his cave.

To Wish This TINITA TIKARAM
Holling passes out eggs.

Coolin Medley THE CHIEFTANS
Maurice plays the bagpipes.

"THE FINAL FRONTIER"

Running Behind TRACY LAWRENCE
Jesse the Bear is dead.

Imperial Hotel
Japanese tourists arrive in Cicely.

Don't Give Your Heart to a Rambler TRAVIS TRITT
Maggie shows Ruth-Anne the package.

English Tea Room
Chris reads from "Paddle to the Sea."

Honeymoon Suite BYRON BERLINE
The boys reassemble Jesse's skeleton.

Pure Chintz
The group decides what to put in the box.

Layin' Back
Holling returns from Widowmaker Cave.

Caribbean Blue ENYA
Chris finishes reading "Paddle to the Sea" and the package is on its way.

"IT HAPPENED IN JUNEAU"

Siegfried and Isolde—Act 1 (WAGNER)
Bernard arrives in town.

I'm in the Mood For Love
Dr. Linda Volpe hits on Joel.

Am I Blue?
Linda continues to flirt with Joel.

The Girl From Ipanema
Maggie and Joel have breakfast together.

I Shot the Sheriff
Joel turns down Linda's advances.

Toy Cows in Africa CHANCE
Chris and Bernard dream about Africa.

"OUR WEDDING"

Solar Sex Panel LITTLE VILLAGE

She Took It Like a Man CONFEDERATE RAILROAD
Maggie is uncomfortable seeing Joel in Holling's bar.

Jelly's Blues
Semanski talks to Maurice.

River of Tears BONNIE RAITT
Shelly puts umbrellas on cupcakes.

Poor Butterfly BENNY GOODMAN
Bachelor party!

The Four Seasons: Spring (VIVALDI)
Bridal Shower!

There'll Be Some Changes Made BENNY GOODMAN
Bachelor party continues...

The Four Seasons: Winter (VIVALDI)
Shelly hands out toilet paper.

I Surrender, Dear BENNY GOODMAN
Joel and Maurice smoke cigars.

The Four Seasons: Autumn (VIVALDI)
Ruth-Anne wraps Maggie a bridal gown out of toilet paper.

"CICELY"

Each Night at Nine FLOYD TILLMAN
Joel nearly hits Ned with his truck.

The Butterfly SHOW'S CAST
The fiddlers in the bar play.

Nearer My God to Thee SHOW'S CAST
Woman sings Bible song.

The Chandler's Wife SHOW'S CAST
Drunk men sing.

Intermezzo Sinfonica *from Cavalleria Rusticana* (MASCAGNI)
Cicely dances.

1992/93 SEASON

"NORTHWEST PASSAGES"

The Bird Dealer *from* *The Magic Flute* (MOZART)
Maggie and Ruth-Anne talk about birthdays and babies.

Queen of Memphis CONFEDERATE RAILROAD
Maggie sits at the bar and talks about her birthday.

Time Flies SASS JORDAN
Marilyn asks Chris to teach her to drive.

Grand River BYRON BERLINE
Maggie convinces a camper to move his campsite.

Let Old Mother Nature Have Her Way CARL SMITH
Joel and Ed drive to save Maggie.

Layin' Back
Maurice and Holling chat in the bar.

Unfinished Blues BYE BYE BLUES
Ruth-Anne smashes Maurice's tape recorder.

Happy Birthday STEVIE WONDER
Joel visits Maggie in the hospital.

"MIDNIGHT SUN"

Glow Worm THE MILLS BROTHERS
A basketball bounces through town.

Badi, Badi *from* *Don Giovanni* (MOZART)
Gillis visits Ruth-Anne's store.

Alma Mater
Bernard talks about Gillis's fashions.

Roll Along Kentucky Moon LEON REDBONE
Joel sketches a gameplan, Shelly practices her cheers.

Saturday Game
Joel reads "Casey at the Bat."

The Bed You Made For Me HIGHWAY 101
Holling and Shelly talk.

Won't You Let Me Go BUCKWHEAT ZYDECO

Don't Mind If I Do GEORGE STRAIT
Gillis dances with Ruth-Anne.

"NOTHING'S PERFECT"

I Heard a Juke Box Playing KITTY WELLS
Chris runs over a dog.

Wie Stark Ist Nicht from *The Magic Flute* (MOZART)
Ed helps Maurice move furniture.

My Next Broken Heart BROOKS AND DUNN
Joel talks to Chris at the bar.

If the Walls Could Talk SKEW SISKIN
Rolf dances in The Brick.

Mean Greens THE ROCK BOX

Darn That Dream
Amy has dinner in Chris's trailer.

Sonata in C minor (SCARLATTI)
Chris tells Ruth-Anne he killed Amy's bird.

You Go to My Head CHET BAKER
Chris tells Amy that Pete is dead.

Sonata in A Major (MOZART)
Rolf packs up the clock.

Inchworm DANNY KAYE
Amy calculates Pi on her computer; Ed edits his film.

"HEROES"

If You Take Me Back BIG JOE AND HIS WASHBOARDS
Chris and Maggie talk by the lake.

Don't Be Cruel CHEAP TRICK
Brad walks into Ruth-Anne's store.

Good Work BO DEANS
Maurice and Holling talk in the bar.

Swing Low, Sweet Chariot ERIC CLAPTON
Chris talks to Tooley's dead body.

Old Time Rock and Roll BOB SEGER
Dead Tooley sings at The Last Supper Club.

Big Big Man BEAT FARMERS
Shelly says Goodbye to Brad.

A Whiter Shade of Pale PROCOL HARUM
Tooley is flung into the lake.

"BLOWING BUBBLES"

On the Sunny Side of the Street LIONEL HAMPTON
Ed drives to Mike's house.

Italian Concerto in F (BACH)
Ed brings groceries to Mike.

I Can't Give You Anything But Love BENNY GOODMAN
Matthew surprises Ruth-Anne.

Symphony No. 5 (BEETHOVEN)
Mike cleans his windows.

Quartet No. 68 (HAYDN)
Mike gives Maggie a tour of the bubble.

Partita No. 1 in B-Major (BACH)
Maggie and Mike picnic in the bubble.

Ghost City
Ruth-Anne tells Maurice to leave her son alone.

Boot Scootin' Boogie BROOKS AND DUNN
Matthew watches the stock report on TV, Joel and Maggie shoot some pool.

Sonata in B-Flat No. 396 (SCARLATTI)
Maggie tries to convince Mike to take a walk.

On the Sunny Side of the Street LIONEL HAMPTON
Mike wears Maurice's spacesuit.

"ON YOUR OWN"

Heartaches by the Numbers DWIGHT YOAKAM
Shelly talks to Mummenschanz.

Theme and Variations (MOZART)
Maggie and Mike talk about the environment.

Rue Partisienne
Ed dreams he wins the Film Institute Awards.

Rue St. Michel
Ed sees Fellini.

Stabat Mater
Mike and Maggie work in the Bubble.

That's Amore DEAN MARTIN
Mike and Maggie walk down the road together.

"THE BAD SEED"

Uptown Downtown CHRIS CHESTNUTT
Jackie walks into the bar looking for Holling.

Queen of Memphis CONFEDERATE RAILROAD
Jackie shows Holling proof he is her dad.

A Hundred Years From Now TRAVIS TRITT
Jackie and Shelly shoot pool.

Somewhere Tonight HIGHWAY 101
Holling and Jackie argue.

Palm Leaf Rag
Chris talks on the radio as Jackie picks Ed's pocket.

Born to Lose
Chris gives Ed advice.

The Whiskey Ain't Workin' TRAVIS TRITT
Shelly and Holling talk in the bar.

Glory Roadway
Holling asks Jackie to leave.

Lay My Love BRIAN ENO
Ed and Chris dance with the cranes.

"THANKSGIVING"

Lambeth Walk DJANGO REINHARDT
Main Street: The town prepares for the Thanksgiving Day Parade.

Over the River and Through the Woods
Chris talks about Thanksgiving on the air.

Let Old Mother Nature Have Her Way

Blue Ridge Party
Everyone talks about Thanksgiving.

Autumn Leaves
Joel shops in Ruth-Anne's store.

Symphony No. 54—First Movement (HAYDN)
Maggie and Mike talk.

Flight of the Cosmic Hippo BELA FLECK
Joel dreams of Sisyphus.

Excuse Me (I Think I've Got a Heartache) THE MAVERICKS
Maggie and Mike talk again.

Sonata in C-Minor (SCARLATTI)
Ed and Mike talk in the Bubble.

Cabaret LOUIS ARMSTRONG
The town has its Thanksgiving Day Parade.

"DO THE RIGHT THING"

Baby It's a Crime THE BLACK SORROWS
Jason inspects The Brick.

I'll See You in My Dreams JAN GARBER
Maggie brings mail to Chris.

Baby, I'm in Love With You RICKY SKAGGS
Holling suggests Shelly ask Jason to the movies.

"CRIME AND PUNISHMENT"

Born to Lose
Semanski arrests Chris.

Rock My Baby SHENANDOAH
Joel and Holling talk in The Brick.

Nocturne No. 2 (CHOPIN)
Maurice asks Mike to represent Chris.

Whiskey If She Were a Woman HIGHWAY 101
Shelly and Ed talk about Chris' fate.

Brandenburg Concerto—Allegro Movement (BACH)
The Judge and Ruth-Anne talk about books.

If I Could Bottle This Up PAUL OVERSTREET
Maurice and Holling watch Semanski eat.

Under a Stormy Sky DANIEL LANOIS

Won't You Let Me Go? BUCKWHEAT ZYDECO
Holling throws a party for Chris.